"Karen Wingate's *Gra*
pause and consider Go
encouragement? Do yc
like God does? *Grateful Heart* will fan the flame of gratitude in
your heart."

—**John and Angel Beeson**, pastor and counselor, and authors of
Trading Faces: Removing the Masks That Hide Your God-Given Identity

"The Bible calls us to live with a constant attitude of gratitude
toward God, yet we live in a culture that fosters entitlement and
discontent. . . . Karen Wingate opens our eyes to the infinite
reasons for gratitude all around us. This book will shift your
perspective."

—**Kathy Howard**, speaker, Bible teacher,
and author of the Deep Rooted devotional series

"There is a richness we may often miss in the simple tasks and
observations that make up our days. Karen Wingate makes the
seemingly mundane meaningful in her new book, *Grateful Heart*.
From cookware to pimentos to pick-up service, the author helps
us pause and consider God's hand in every little aspect of life.
Each devotional reading will inspire readers to give thanks in all
things."

—**Janet Holm McHenry**, author of 27 books, including
Looking Up! Finding Joy as You Read and Pray through the Bible

"This book is filled with Christ-centered insights that cause the
reader to give deeper thought and express greater gratitude for God's
presence and the miraculous work He is accomplishing all around
us. Your heart will be encouraged and your faith will be strength-
ened as you apply the biblical wisdom found in *Grateful Heart*."

—**John Stange**, author of *Dwell on These Things*
and host of the *Chapter-a-Day Audio Bible* podcast

"'In everything give thanks.' This is one mindset in Scripture that can seem impossible to keep. In *everything*? What about the death of a loved one? Life-changing debilitating disease? Rejection by family or friends? Times when life seems to be falling apart? There are few people who have found the ability to be thankful at all times. Karen Wingate is one of them. . . . I highly recommend this great devotional!"

—**Julie Zine Coleman**, managing editor for Arise Daily and author of *On Purpose: Understanding God's Freedom for Women* and *Unexpected Love: God's Heart Revealed in Jesus' Conversations with Women*

Grateful Heart

60 REASONS
TO GIVE THANKS
IN ALL THINGS

Karen Wingate

Our Daily Bread
Publishing.

Requests for permission to quote from this book should be directed to: Permissions Department, Our Daily Bread Publishing, PO Box 3566, Grand Rapids, MI 49501, or contact us by email at permissionsdept@odb.org.

Scripture quotations, unless otherwise indicated, are taken from the Holy Bible, New International Version®, NIV®. Copyright © 1973, 1978, 1984, 2011 by Biblica, Inc.™ Used by permission of Zondervan. All rights reserved worldwide. www.zondervan.com.

Scripture quotations marked NASB are taken from the New American Standard Bible®, copyright © 1960, 1971, 1977, 1995, 2020 by The Lockman Foundation. Used by permission. All rights reserved. lockman.org.

Scripture quotations marked NLT are taken from the *Holy Bible*, New Living Translation, copyright © 1996, 2004, 2015 by Tyndale House Foundation. Used by permission of Tyndale House Publishers, Carol Stream, Illinois 60188. All rights reserved.

Interior design by Michael J. Williams

ISBN: 978-1-64070-369-8

Library of Congress Cataloging-in-Publication Data Available

Printed in the United States of America
25 26 27 28 29 30 31 32 / 8 7 6 5 4 3 2 1

Contents

Contents

Acknowledgments
What I'm Thankful For

What would a book on gratitude be without that section we typically call *acknowledgments*?

What am I thankful for?

I'm thankful for the little things of life that make it possible for me to do what I love. Things like pens and paper, the voice memo app on my phone, and my laptop. I'm thankful for coffee, chocolate, heat patches, and walks in perfect spring Arizona weather that kept my body functioning so I could write.

But most of all, I'm thankful for the people God has placed in my life who remind me daily that every big project takes a team of gifted people to make it happen.

I'm thankful for members of my church family who asked every Sunday, "How's the book coming?" For those who smiled when I said, "Great!" and hugged me when I said, "Bad week."

I'm thankful for my pastor, Jesse Craig, and his partnership with the Holy Spirit in his choice of sermon topics. Countless Sundays, without knowing what I was doing, Jesse preached on exactly the topic I planned to write on during the following week.

His voice and wisdom guided my thinking in a number of places within these pages.

I'm thankful for the dozens of friends on Facebook who answered my zany questions and had the decency to not ask, "Where are you going with this one?"

I'm thankful for my agent, Linda Glaz, who says I'm a model of perseverance. Hearing her say that has kept me going more than a few times. I couldn't let her down, could I? Linda, you are the poster child of *Don't Give Up*, for you refuse to give up on any of your clients, and we so appreciate you.

I'm thankful for my mother and for the Holy Spirit of God who lives within her. Several times, through the fog of her developing dementia, she has given me wise counsel and input, words that I knew were beyond her mental struggle.

I'm thankful for my sweet husband who, in his prayer at the breakfast table, prayed for my writing every single morning. Oh, and the coffee and back rubs were nice too.

I'm thankful for Kelly, my accountability partner, who, well, kept me accountable. Each week, Kelly and I share our goals for the next week and check on each other midweek. Kelly is stellar at giving lots of grace and gentle nudges if I overplan, and good suggestions for managing better the next time.

Finally, I'm thankful for my prayer team of fourteen women who, despite their own share of "worst moments," prayed faithfully for me throughout the writing of this book. You ladies all belong in my Picture Gallery of Faith. You've shown me portraits of resilient faith, and I'm so grateful for your courage, hope, and joy through whatever life has thrown at you.

Introduction

A Fresh Look at Gratitude

Give thanks in all circumstances; for this is
God's will for you in Christ Jesus.

1 Thessalonians 5:18

Legally blind since birth, I underwent surgery in my midfifties that unexpectedly gave me better vision than I'd ever had in my life. Gratitude came easily as I explored my world for all the things I'd missed seeing throughout my life. I blabbed about what I could see for the first time to anyone who wanted to listen and to a few who didn't. Autumn leaves, snow, and flowers of multiple hues—the world was a beautiful place.

God and I had a lot of catching up to do. Each new sighting taught me something more about my Savior, and I collected my treasure stones in a book called *With Fresh Eyes*. I invited readers to sit with me in the theater of my new experience to enjoy all those wonders I was seeing for the first time.

Occasionally, when I came up for air, I would catch wistful happiness etched on several friends' faces. Curbing my enthusiasm, I started listening to their difficult stories. They were thankful

11

for what I could see with new eyes, but inwardly they struggled to peek around the boulders in their own lives. I had gained new sight; they were losing theirs.

My doctors and I knew, however, that the results of the surgery were both tenuous and temporary. My new visual acuity was still far from the normal 20/20 vision that others enjoy, and the procedure was done in only one eye, leaving my other eye still mostly useless. It had brought improvement to only two of my long list of eye dysfunctions and had been risky at that—it could have destroyed my fragile eyesight. And while I see better now than I ever have before, the health of my left eye is unstable. It wouldn't take much for me to lose the rest of my vision.

Other friends faced different kinds of loss: divorce, cancer, chronic pain, financial woes, and mundane moments of care for a child with multiple disabilities. "Why isn't God doing anything for me?" one ventured to ask.

But the Bible says in 1 Thessalonians 5:18 that we are to be thankful in all circumstances. And Paul emphasizes the command: "For this is God's will for you in Christ Jesus." How do we obey the "all" of that instruction? Can we be thankful on both cloudy and sunny days? Can we stay thankful when we're losing instead of gaining? Can I be as joy filled if my eyesight diminishes?

I decided to search the Bible for the secret of thankfulness in all circumstances. The pages of this book contain what I discovered.

I was amazed at the results of my search. God's world contains far more sensory data than I could begin to process in any given day. I can't possibly see, hear, touch, taste, or smell everything God has put within my reach, even if I had a hundred days to meticulously study my surroundings.

Life, even with its tragedies, has fullness and purpose when I peer through God's viewfinder.

Stories of God's power and provision in the past remind me that today's difficulty is not the end of the story, and I will eventually say, "See what God did!"

Through my new life in Christ, God offers me an array of spiritual blessings that nothing on this earth can ever snatch from me.

God has lined my life path with supportive people, all of whom are part of God's plan for me.

When the worst of this world shatters my dreams, God still walks with me, empowering me to meld the bits of brokenness together into stained-glass artistry that honors Him and allows me to emerge on the other side of life—victorious.

Whatever circumstance you and I might face, we can stay grateful. Life is stuffed with more gratitude prompts than you can fit inside a twenty-four-pound Thanksgiving turkey. You just have to look for them.

I invite you to open your eyes to God's expansive goodness. Search for the gemstones. Remember the bright moments of the past—the times when God helped you find the right street when you were hopelessly lost or sent a friend when your grief was overwhelming. Look for where God is in the moment—in the bright green of leaves or the crispness of a good cup of black tea. Find gratitude in what you have today rather than worry about what you might not have in the future. Examine God's best plans concealed within the things often considered by the world as unpleasant. And, most of all, let's you and I find contentment in our relationship with Jesus—that if we lost everything, He would be enough.

Gratitude in all circumstances *is* possible. In fact, thanksgiving is a key to survival through the tough moments. Gratitude can coexist with the worst of times because God's nature never changes, and His blessings reflect and reveal His unchanging, everlasting character.

Will you come with me? Let's go on a discovery trip to search for God's goodness that shines like gold amidst the dirty smudges of our messy lives. Let's find out together that it really is possible to be thankful in all circumstances.

PART ONE

Gifts in Plain Sight

How abundant are the good things
that you have stored up for those who fear you,
that you bestow in the sight of all,
on those who take refuge in you.

PSALM 31:19

God lines our daily journey with gifts for us to see at close range. We can find joy and gratitude in the everyday small gifts that we already have.

1

The Sun

The faithful love of the LORD never ends!
His mercies never cease.
Great is his faithfulness;
his mercies begin afresh each morning.

LAMENTATIONS 3:22–23 NLT

Normally I find immense peace and joy in a Christmas Eve service. But one particular year when we attended services with our daughter and family, my visual hypersensitivity to light glare and flicker in a new environment caused me to flee the auditorium before the candlelight portion of the service began. In that moment, I wished I could have walked away as easily from the overwhelming concerns of my heart as I did from the annoying flicker of a candle.

As I left the auditorium and entered the lobby, the church logo displayed on the opposite wall caught my eye. The name of the church, *Del Sol*, was printed beneath a stylized outline of a sun. The drawing, my limited Spanish vocabulary, and an affirmation from Google Translate interpreted the name: *Of the Sun.*

Why would a Christ-centered church align itself with something from creation? My overactive brain quickly deduced the answer.

The sun always shines. It is so dependable that our newspapers and electronic device apps tell us exactly when it will rise and set in any given location. Every day, the sun follows a path through the sky, shedding light and warmth on the earth. Even the psalmist described the sun this way: "It rises at one end of the heavens and makes its circuit to the other; nothing is deprived of its warmth" (Psalm 19:6).

The sun never detours. Man can do nothing to destroy it, for it will continue to rise every morning and set every evening until Jesus comes again. We can count on it. See how the sun is an appropriate name to represent a group of God's people? What a wonderful way to remind worshipers of God's faithfulness whenever they left any group gathering.

"What are you talking about?" you might protest. "The sun hasn't shone in my locale in several weeks."

I hear you. I've lived long enough in the desert southwest to know that people who live here don't like cloud cover. We prefer our sunshine. Unless clouds bring a good healthy rain to settle the dust or create photo-worthy sunsets, we don't do clouds. A day-long cloud cover makes many of us grumpy. However, we need rain to give the earth nourishment, so bring it on—but make it snappy and then let's get back to our regularly scheduled sunshine. After all, we like to boast, the sun shines three-hundred-fifty-plus days a year here, and we'd like to keep it that way.

If you live in a cloudier climate, you may now laugh at me. Besides, you and I both know that three-hundred-fifty-day average stuff is not quite accurate.

Tucson residents may say the sun shines three hundred fifty days a year. And those living in Seattle may bemoan that the sun shines only one hundred fifty-two days a year. The problem is in the words *sun shines*. I'm word picking, I know. But the sun shines three-hundred-sixty-five days a year no matter where you live. It shines every day. You may not see the sun on a particular day, but the sun is still there, ready to emerge when the mist of cloud moves aside.

Our lives depend on the warmth and light of the sun. If the sun didn't shine, our earth would be completely dark and deathly cold. Planet Earth suspends in just the right place in the solar system to sustain human life. Too close to the sun, we would burn up. Farther out, we would freeze.

God said, "As long as the earth endures, seedtime and harvest, cold and heat, summer and winter, day and night will never cease" (Genesis 8:22). Seasons will continue as long as the earth remains. They will not stop. That's God solemn promise to us.

What a relief. When the world seems like it's spinning out of control and you're tempted to wonder if God has lost His grip, one look at the rising sun (or imagining it behind the clouds) can remind you that God is still in charge. His sunlight will always begin your day, with or without clouds. As Lamentations 3:22–23 assures us, God's faithfulness is great, and His mercy gets a fresh start every morning.

The sun guides our trek toward gratitude in all things, for it is the first of many prompts that remind us of the gifts from God that surround us every day, despite our current circumstances. You and I can face each new day confident and grateful that God is and will be as dependable and consistent as the rising sun. Just as His created sun is always there to replenish light and warmth, His presence is always available to guide, provide, and protect us through any storm-filled day.

We can count on it.

GRATITUDE PROMPT

Look toward the sun. Thank God for His constant show of faithfulness as displayed through the rhythms and seasons of the earth. Thank Him for the promise of His faithfulness in your own life.

2

Birds

Are not five sparrows sold for two pennies? Yet
not one of them is forgotten by God.

LUKE 12:6

After a full day of work, I hovered over my sink, scrubbing
vegetables for supper. As I flexed my shoulder muscles and
rotated my stiff neck, my eyes caught a fluttering of red outside
the kitchen window. I stilled. It was a robin!

With my moderate vision loss, I rarely catch sight of any bird.
I've learned to keep an assistive device called a monocular on my
windowsill so I can get a closer view of life outside my kitchen
window. My hand moved with stealth toward the monocular,
furiously hoping my motion wouldn't scare off the robin. It didn't,
and for a few sweet moments, I watched his every move, realizing
why many people find bird-watching a fascinating hobby.

No wonder the colloquial nickname for robins is Robin Red
Breast. This particular guy didn't have the red color of a stop sign
like I'd imagined; it was more of a burnished orange or a flaming red, accompanied by a lower white underbelly and speckled,
fawn-colored top feathers. I was glad that robins like to forage
for insects and seeds at ground level, for I could easily track the

little bird as it burrowed its beak in the wet early-evening grass and then cocked its head and ruffled its feathers.

My new little friend looked so relaxed, unperturbed, and comfortable in his limited world. I thought of the beautiful music he and other birds produced each morning. I smiled as I remembered hearing the fluttering and fussing at a bird feeder as its various customers jockeyed for position but easily forgave and forgot the next time they came to feed. Oh, to be as tranquil as a bird and not hold grudges from the past!

Spotting the robin brought a flurry of questions about bird life to my mind, for which I found ready answers on the Internet. The world hosts over ten thousand species of birds, similar in their basic shape and flight design but all incredibly unique and amazingly detailed. God reserved an entire day of creation for fish and fowl, designing everything from the mighty eagle to the tiny, two-inch-long bee hummingbird. God draped the birds in splendored color that almost hurts the eyes with its brilliance: the multicolored macaw and the solid colors of the blue jay, yellow finch, and red cardinal. The world contains so many species that bird-watchers catalog their findings, always hoping to find that one elusive type they have not yet seen.

And then there is the sparrow. The common, ordinary house sparrow. So common, bird-watchers mention their presence as an afterthought, preferring to get more excited over a yellow-bellied sapsucker or an indigo bunting. Dressed in browns and grays, a sparrow blends into the background of trees and ground cover. Sparrows are just . . . there.

Yet of all the variety of birds, Jesus chose the sparrow as an example of His watchful care over us. Sparrows may be common enough to slip off our radar, but they are never forgotten by God. When Jesus reminded His listeners of God's awareness of the sparrows, He went on to add, "Don't be afraid; you are worth more than many sparrows" (Luke 12:7).

I wonder if God created an abundance of sparrows so He could surround His human creation with the daily reminder, *I'm here. I see you. I know what is going on with you, and you are not alone. You are not too ordinary for Me to remember you.*

God has filled the sky's amphitheater with a never-ending chorus of birdsong, singing sweet peace over the turbulent souls of His beloved children. He gives us the beauty of bird life so we can pause, praise, and find peace in the middle of busy, stress-filled days. We may need to stop what we're doing, look away from our workload, and zoom in on what He has made. Thankfully, we never have to look very far. A reminder of God's love might be as ordinary as a sparrow who does nothing more than exist, trusting in God's care and singing the song the Creator entrusted to it.

If you enjoy bird-watching, I hope you find that new variety you've been looking for. But let me suggest an additional strategy. The next time you pick up your binoculars, look for the bird that is always there, whether a sparrow, starling, dove, or other kind common to your region. Marvel in its layers of variegated color. Watch it move from a perch to a flight take-off. Note how it spreads its wings and folds them like a Japanese fan when it lands. Watch how it interacts with other birds. Listen for its unique song.

That bird may be common, ordinary, and overlooked. But it's living the life God intended for it. Nothing will happen to that tiny bird without the knowledge of its loving Creator. As God cares for it, so He will care for you.

GRATITUDE PROMPT

The next time you see a bird, any bird, take note of its physical detail and life habits. Thank God for His marvelous gift of birds that serves as a memento of His awareness of and care for you.

3

Vanilla Beans

Everything that lives and moves about will be food for you.
Just as I gave you the green plants, I now give you everything.

GENESIS 9:3

My family loves homemade, hand-cranked vanilla ice cream.
It's more than a tradition. It's a time-honored ritual.
When we get together, summer or winter, we dig out Grandma's
secret recipe, check our supply of rock salt, and soak the wooden
bucket. Back in the day, vanilla was cheap, especially if we got it
in quart-sized bottles from over the border in Mexico. The cook
would add a generous one-fourth cup to the one-gallon canister,
take a deep whiff, and then add a splash more.

There was a certain pecking order to the making of our long-
held tradition. One of the adults or my oldest brother would do
the cranking. The youngest child—that would be me—sat on
the towel-covered bucket to steady it. My reward was to lick the
dasher while standing in the middle of the backyard when the
ice cream was ready. At age thirty-five, when I returned home for
my grandmother's funeral, I still had the job of sitting on that
bucket. That time, I declined the dasher.

I still love the taste and smell of vanilla. To me, it is one of life's
best pleasures. But I learned recently that vanilla does not come

to its customers easily. Cultivators must either wait for the elusive *Melipona* bee to do the job of pollination or hand pollinate the rare vanilla orchid flowers themselves. The fragile orchids bloom for only twenty-four hours every year, making natural vanilla even more elusive and expensive. No wonder modern food chemists have concocted synthetic vanilla.

Here's the amazing part to me. Vanilla beans—and coffee and cacao beans, for that matter—were on the earth for centuries before people discovered how to morph them into an edible form. Several more centuries elapsed before producers fine-tuned the process and made them available for mass production. God created and placed those treasured beans within plain sight.

It's easy to reason that humanity's cleverness empowered us to figure out how to process these plants. But wait a minute. Where did the beans originate? Who created the beans? Of course, God did. Our knowledge and creativity to maneuver the beans into a usable product came from somewhere too—God himself. It all came from God.

Genesis 1:26 outlines God's plan: people would have the right, privilege, and responsibility to manage the earth and its resources. That includes devising new ways to responsibly oversee the use of earth's products. Part of the joy of human history is the innovations that manage and repurpose our natural resources. Humanity's incredible quest to discover and invent has led to phenomenal products, things once unheard of but now so common we take them for granted.

All of earth is ours to discover, cultivate, and develop to make it better. The Lord simply asks that we do all of it with a thankful heart, acknowledging that it started with Him (1 Timothy 4:3–5). The first step of the gratitude process is to give credit where credit is due—to the One who designed and continues to provide the gift.

So the next time you or I dip into a bowl of ice cream— commercial or hand-cranked—we can savor the centuries-long ingenuity it took to figure out things like separating cream from milk, growing vanilla beans, cultivating sugar, and mixing it all together in a thousand different combinations to make a wonderful and nourishing dessert. We can thank God for designing us with unlimited creativity and insatiable curiosity. We can relish the family memories that swirl around us whenever we get together to enjoy special treats and treasured moments. And we can find utter delight in the fact that God would design a rare plant that brings people so much pleasure.

Go enjoy. Your ice cream is melting!

GRATITUDE PROMPT

Think of a food you particularly enjoy. Thank God for the creation of that food, the wisdom and knowledge He's given food scientists to cultivate it, and His design of taste buds so you can enjoy it.

4

Furry Friends

God made the wild animals according to their kinds,
the livestock according to their kinds, and all the
creatures that move along the ground according to
their kinds. And God saw that it was good.

GENESIS 1:25

After losing her vision from diabetic retinopathy, my fourth-grade Sunday school teacher, Dorothy—or "Dot," as the adults called her—lost no time in applying for a guide dog. Two months later, Gary, a beautiful yellow Labrador retriever, slept and snored under Dot's pew every Sunday morning.

Dot still wanted to teach Sunday school. Her group of children became the largest class in our small church, and church leadership was never sure if the children came for the dog or the Bible stories. No matter. Dot had strict rules. They had to listen to the lesson, and then she allowed ten minutes at the end for "Gary time." Children heard about Jesus, and that's what mattered most.

Therapy and service dogs have some inherent traits that equip them to connect to people in need in a special way. While their service needs to be developed and targeted through training, not all dogs have that special connection, says Mildred, who owns Max, another therapy dog.

Max was different, even at eight months old. While most boxers are rather exuberant, Max was always chill. After testing and training, Max and Mildred were licensed to take Max into rehab centers and schools to interact with adults and children. One of Max's greatest accomplishments was to befriend children who were fearful of dogs. His quiet, full-acceptance-of-the-children personality made them reach out to him, read stories to him, and give him hugs and treats.

My interaction with my Welsh corgi is less noteworthy but still telling. Tuesday (yes, that was her name) figured out my work schedule. Her herding instinct, distinctive in Welsh corgis, drove her to sit by my office door each morning at nine, emitting soft woofs. When I finally entered the room, coffee cup in hand, and sat at my desk, Tuesday would settle herself in the crawl space on top of my feet for her first morning nap. I was trapped into working! When we went for our midmorning walk, her big-dog mentality in a small dog's body would face down dogs twice her size as she inserted herself between them and me.

Our pets give us companionship, provide protection, and make us laugh. They give us something to care about when we have the need to nurture and feel useful. I've heard a dog makes for the best house security system. And, like Gary and Max, dogs have proved themselves valuable in roles as service and therapy dogs.

God made them to be that way.

Genesis 1:25 makes a distinction between wild animals and cattle or livestock as the New International Version, New American Standard Bible, and other versions translate the Hebrew word, God specifically created a separate classification of animals that would be compatible and friendly toward people. These animals over time have not evolved to a higher level, and they are not the next step down from humans. From the beginning of time, God created a classification of animals with special abilities so they could serve people.

Within the category of domesticated animals, God gifted each species with special skills. Draft horses pull heavy loads, oxen aid in farming, and donkeys and camels act as cargo carriers. Homing pigeons deliver messages, canaries alert miners to toxic chemicals, and for centuries, horses served as human transportation.

Perhaps dogs are the most versatile in their usefulness. They guard, protect, herd other animals, aid in hunting, sniff out bombs and drugs, find missing people, rescue drowning swimmers, and guide the blind. And God gives special gifts to specific dogs like Gary, Max, and Tuesday and connects them with specific people who need their love, faithfulness, protection, and unwavering acceptance.

When I was a pastor's wife, I watched my dogs welcome visitors at the door, then lie at their feet and lick tears from their hands as the conversation went deep and personal. The dog's acceptance softened our visitors' hearts and made them feel safe enough to trust. After my guests left with renewed hope and peace, I rewarded my dogs with treats and told them they were good "Jesus helpers."

While God never meant for our furry friends to replace His presence in our lives, the Lord uses them as part of His answer to our pleas for protection, peace, and nurturing. They become a micro-glimpse of God's love and faithfulness toward us.

Put simply, our animal friends are a blessing from God. They are both His gift to us and His provision for us. He planned it that way. Even before He created man and woman, God set the classification of domesticated animals in place for our blessing and benefit, and He gifted certain ones for special tasks.

Animals are one more gift from the hands of a loving heavenly Father.

GRATITUDE PROMPT

Do you own an animal? Snag a treat and share it with your furry friend, thanking God for the ways He has used this animal to bless your life. And if you see a service or therapy dog in public, quietly thank the Lord for placing that dog in his owner's life.

5

Baby Giggles

Our mouths were filled with laughter,
our tongues with songs of joy.
Then it was said among the nations,
"The Lord has done great things for them."
PSALM 126:2

I couldn't help myself. My laughter erupted like someone had turned on a water spigot full throttle. It came from somewhere deep, a pleasure place located between my heart and my gut that's reserved for moments of spontaneous delight.

It was my grandson's doing.

His good mama, willing to forego all that's proper, had taught him to blow milk bubbles in his sippy cup. The nearly two-year-old little boy thought that was great fun. His giggles burst forth in a belly laugh, spewing milk over his mouth and down the cup. At Mama's encouragement, he tried again but couldn't because he was laughing too hard. And my daughter had the presence of mind—or gall, if you will—to video the moment and send the link to the grandparents.

We laughed with him. Mature-thinking adults laughing over the sound of milk bubbles. We kept chuckling as he found glee over the tickling sensation, the peculiar sounds, and the shock of a popped bubble. We called for encore videos so we could enjoy what else made him laugh. Obligingly, his parents would impulsively set him up to laugh so all of us could laugh with him. Tickling, roughhousing, the joy of learning how to operate the motion sensor on the trash can lid, or hearing us laugh first turned on that giggle machine.

And we all passed the bucket of smiles that relieved the day's tension and stress.

Laughter feels good. I'm glad God thought up the idea of laughter. Since He designed us to laugh, He must have intended for us to find delight within His world and enjoy the life He's given us. Not a quiet, reverent, "Thank you, Lord, for what thou hast made," but a belly wrenching, explosive, "Wow, God. You did this? That is awesome!" kind of joy.

For that matter, God made all our feelings: sad, happy, angry, cautious, and so many more. Yet, like other parts of life, we've corrupted the expressions of our emotions and found ways to mismanage our reactions. Laughter morphs into a weapon used to scorn and belittle others. Sadness can turn to despair. Righteous anger, which could motivate us to take action in overcoming evil, corrodes into destructive violence. Humans have become masterful at using our emotions to manipulate others.

That's one reason why I love baby giggles. They're innocent, uninhibited, and without guile. Society has not yet had a chance to put parameters around when it's acceptable for them to laugh and when it isn't. The child doesn't think through life-altering decisions—what will others think of me if I dissolve into a hysterical giggle fit? They just laugh. The giggles aren't scripted. *See bubbles, will laugh. I hear laughter, I'll laugh too.* They're spontaneous, impulsive, done from a simple, it-feels-so-good-to-laugh frame of mind.

Baby giggles are untarnished joy. My grandson is discovering the world for the first time. Everything is new and exciting. He's spending those first few precious years learning, processing, categorizing, and studying every single bit of life—from the movement of a bug to a bubble of milk. That little boy is in high gear for discovery and it's all so fascinating, awesome, and exciting.

Even better, baby giggles are infectious, inviting us adults to shuck off our concerns—was that even funny?—and laugh. I dare you. Try to frown while watching a two-year-old throw back his head, squint his eyes, and let it rip. Your lips twitch. You can't contain it. And we discover that even on our worst days, a child's laugh has softened the harshness of life.

Isn't it lovely that God created us to laugh? You and I are a long way past the baby stage of discovery. But God's gift of laughter still tucks itself deep within us. God intends it to be an outlet for expressing our deepest joy at the world's wonders and life's more satisfying moments.

What brings you deep-down delight? The beauty of a certain part of creation. A shared moment of contentment with family and longtime friends as you remember the past. Watching the uninhibited play of children.

What about an incredulous laugh that bursts forth when you hear that God has done the impossible once more. A report of cancer remission from the doctor. A check in the mail when you feared you couldn't pay your electric bill. Or the good news of someone who you never expected would yield to God's ways coming to faith in Jesus.

Do you need to laugh again? No matter how hard life has become, laughter still exists, and laughter is good. God wants you to use His invention of laughter—to use it well and use it often. My friend, if you need to rediscover the kind of laughter that fills you with deep joy, find something today to laugh about. Then thank God that He thought up the idea of laughter.

If you have trouble letting the laughter out, find a video of baby giggles.

GRATITUDE PROMPT

Listen for a child's laugh. Thank God for designing laughter and for filling our world with delightful things we can laugh about.

6

Touch

Jesus reached out his hand and touched the
man. "I am willing," he said. "Be clean!"
Immediately he was cleansed of his leprosy.

Matthew 8:3

Not realizing I couldn't see the eye of a needle, my mother felt it was important for me to learn sewing basics. Back in the day before Mother knew about needle threaders, I figured out my own way to get the job done. One day, Mother watched me hold the thread between my thumb and forefinger and then bring the needle down to the thread.

"That's not the way you thread a needle," she scolded.

I wasn't in the habit of being impertinent to my mother, but that day, orneriness ruled. "That's the way I do it." Mother didn't realize I was accomplishing the task 98 percent by touch.

An eye of a needle became my gateway to the discovery of God's gift of touch. A soft brush of my fingers gave me cues and clues when my limited sight failed to deliver what I needed to know. Fingers curled over cup edges announced the water level when it reached the top. A featherweight pressure of my fingertips on a knife blade determined its sharpness without cutting my skin. Much to my husband's dismay, I often walked through the house at night with no lights on. Who needs lights?

My feet, through the soles of my shoes, deciphered stones I could not see. My hands discovered the contours and beard stubble of my beloved's face. "Don't shave yet," I'd beg. "I like feeling your prickles."

The truth is that a blind person has no superpower of highly developed touch. They've merely discovered what belongs to everyone. Fully sighted people have no compelling reason to cultivate what they have. But oh, they are missing out on so much! Touch gives us concrete information about size, shape, texture, and temperature, things we can't always determine by sight.

By itself sight can be deceptive, but touch allows us to confirm what we first see with our eyes. No wonder Jesus invited Thomas to touch His side where Roman soldiers had pieced Him before death (John 20:27). Skin-to-skin contact gave Thomas rock solid proof: yes, this was the same man who had been crucified yet now lived.

In addition to being a source of information and identification, touch and sensory perception give us physical sensations of pain and pleasure. Pain alerts us to seek medical attention for a physical ailment. And pleasure—that intrigues me. God is not a pragmatic God. He specially created our bodies to find pleasure through our five sensory perceptions, especially through the sense of touch.

Humans have learned to use touch as a source of unspoken interaction. The terms "good touch" and "bad touch" denote that emotional communication, for touch can express affection, assurance, control, or anger.

Jesus used the gift of good touch to convey a powerful message in His healing ministry. In New Testament times, when leprosy was common, the Jewish culture had social distancing and quarantining down to a fine art. Lepers had to live in colonies separate from the rest of society. They not only had to stand far away from others; they also had to shout "Unclean! Unclean!" No one wanted to touch a leper.

Imagine how you would feel. You've been deprived of human contact for way too long. And not just because you were separated from society. Since leprosy kills off pain sensors, you wouldn't feel anyone touch you. But you would mentally understand the danger. Your entire being would long for touch yet recoil in fear that the other person would catch your dreaded disease.

Yet Jesus dared to reach out to a leper (Matthew 8:3). His contact communicated two messages: first, one of acceptance. Jesus could have healed without physical connection. Instead he put his hand on a leper, silently communicating His love for the one who stood before Him. *You are worthy. You deserve healing. I care about you, and I want you whole in body and spirit.*

Second, Jesus's touch also spoke of His power. *I have no need to be afraid of you, my friend,* His touch would say. Jesus was God's Son. It was impossible for Him to contract leprosy. The disease had no power over Him. Instead, He had power over the disease.

God's good gifts lie literally at your fingertips. Think about what is within the reach of your touch. The smooth page of paper or cool screen of your device as you read this book. The shoes encompassing your feet and keeping your toes warm. Single strands of hair tickling the sides of your face. The bit of pain as you press a nail into another finger. All these indicate you have both the sensation of touch and the reality of objects to touch.

Through the sense of touch God gave you, you can pass forward Jesus's acceptance and power to those who are hurting. Like Jesus, your touch can say, *I care, you are worthy, and I am not afraid to come close.* All because of what God in His goodness has given you.

GRATITUDE PROMPT

Close your eyes. Discover your tactile world within the reach of your fingers. With each sensation, thank God for creating the sense of touch.

7

Smell

Through Jesus, therefore, let us continually
offer to God a sacrifice of praise—the fruit
of lips that openly profess his name.

HEBREWS 13:15

I have enjoyed making homemade bread since I was a teenager.
I'm not sure what gives me the most pleasure: the feel of the
pliable dough beneath my hands as I mold it into loaves, the
yeasty scent that fills my kitchen in the first ten minutes of baking, or the rapturous look of delight as recipients sniff long and
deep of the still warm bread.

Wouldn't it be wonderful if we could bottle and market the
smell of fresh-baked bread?

We all have our favorite pleasant smells. For many, it is the
scent of cookies fresh from the oven or barbecued meat hot off
the grill. Others find joy in the fragrance of lilacs or gardenias.
Nothing can beat the combination of soap and baby as you nuzzle
your nose into your child's or grandchild's clean neck.

Certain smells elicit more pleasure when we associate them with
memories of past treasured moments. The smell of homemade
bread will forever bring back happy memories of baking for my

family, providing dinner rolls for church functions, and gifting friends with love loafs at Christmas.

God often described His reaction to the Israelites' worship of Him through burnt offerings as an "aroma pleasing to the LORD" (Leviticus 2:2; 4:31). I think the Lord had something more in mind than catching a heavenly whiff of roasting meat. The sacrifices represented His chosen people, who gave their time and resources to draw close to God and worship Him. A people willing to humble themselves, repent of their sins, and acknowledge Him as the one true God.

Since we are no longer under the Levitical law, we don't need animal sacrifices to connect with God. But the writer of Hebrews mentions a different kind of sacrifice that makes God happy: the sacrifice of praise. How is praise a sacrifice? When I honor God for something that has happened, I relinquish my right to take the credit for myself. I exchange time spent celebrating my own accomplishments to honor Him instead. My praise shows I recognize that He is God and I am not. He controls the universe, not me. And when I step to the side, my audience attention turns to the one who has made possible all I have done. God deserves all the praise.

We intensify the scent of our praise when we commend our Lord to others and when we imitate His character. Second Corinthians 2:14 says, "Thanks be to God, who always leads us as captives in Christ's triumphal procession and uses us to spread the aroma of the knowledge of him everywhere." When we profess the name of Christ, walk with Him, and represent who He is through our God-honoring actions, we spread the sweet, alluring smell of God's grace. As God leads us triumphantly through the struggles of this life, our faith and trust in Him are as pleasantly apparent to a watching world as the strong scent of a gardenia. And the Lord smiles with greater delight. The message about Jesus expands, and heaven fills with the beautiful scent, more glorious than any lilac garden or bakery kitchen. Our words of praise and God-honoring actions will fill the world like the best of sweet aromas.

The next time you sniff a flower, inhale the scent of freshly baked chocolate chip cookies, or encounter the smell of salt water on an ocean beach, thank the Lord for creating so many wonderful smells that bring us pleasure. Then ask Him to make your life and testimony about Jesus as pleasantly alluring to Him as those wonderful smells are to you. Our Lord God will be delighted with your gratitude for His good gifts. And He'll do His part to spread the fragrance of your praise far beyond what you could possibly imagine.

GRATITUDE PROMPT

When you next catch a whiff of a favorite smell, breathe deep. Thank God for creating that awesome aroma. Share the moment with someone nearby. Be bold! Give God the credit. Your public praise will fill the air with a sweet perfume for everyone near you to enjoy.

8

Coffee Makers

Satisfy us in the morning with your unfailing love,
that we may sing for joy and be glad all our days.

PSALM 90:14

I awoke one morning, rehashing remnants of a phone conversation from the day before. My caller had been vindictive and judgmental, making demands on me I believed impossible to fulfill. In the early morning dark, I fretted that, with a lack of sleep and this new burden on my mind, I couldn't accomplish the day's responsibilities.

I might as well get up, I thought. Anything to stop the nagging thoughts.

I did what I always do each morning. I headed for my coffee maker, inwardly grumbling at the unfairness of life. But as I settled in my soft blue rocking chair and opened my Bible app, I smiled with pleasure at the sight of my favorite shade of blue and the gurgling of the coffee maker mingled with the patter of a much-needed gentle winter rain on the rooftop.

Now, what was I complaining about?

How rich I was! I held a mug, a birthday present from a good friend. My coffee was a special blend, a gift from my daughter. The winter storm made a down payment on valley rain and mountain snow that makes desert dwellers daydream of springtime trips to see landscapes strewn with belly flowers. I had the Bible available to me in both printed form and smartphone app.

As I read my selected Scripture for that day, God satisfied my need for reassurance about His unfailing love. Things always look worse at night, but when I wake up and find God's love gifts tucked around my house, the joy that infuses me is a better energizer than a shot of espresso.

While we spend the wee hours turning over the problems we face as often as we shift our bodies on an unrelenting mattress, the Lord restocks our morning treasure box. He tucks in new surprises—a beautiful sunrise, a bird's trill, and an excuse to turn on the gas fireplace and feel its warmth. Signs of God's love are there, waiting for us every single morning—sights and sounds that speak to our weary souls and troubled spirits.

The reassurance of His watchful care and provision come in odd disguises: the blessing of coffee makers, gentle rain, electric lights, and sustaining words from His Word. His gifts are not mine to expect or demand. Instead each gift of the morning reminds me to focus in gratitude for what I do have instead of looking toward the empty spots and regretting what I don't have. Appreciation morphs into trust, for if God has provided the abundance of this morning, will He not do so again tomorrow? Will He not continue to fill life with joy throughout the rest of this day? And if He has shown His care through so many delightful little touches, can we not trust Him to take care of the matters that worry our hearts?

The psalmist repeats the wonders of God's morning gifts when he says, "Let the morning bring me word of your unfailing love, for I have put my trust in you. Show me the way I should go, for to you I entrust my life" (Psalm 143:8). Notice how the writer connects gratitude, trust, and the humble request that God take the role of a life coach. If God has proved His love for us yet again in the first light of dawn, we can trust Him for the needs of the rest of the day. And if we can trust Him, we can also request, "Show me the way I should go," confident that He will do it.

Gratitude and trust go together like peanut butter and jelly, milk and cookies, or macaroni and cheese. Saying thanks to God for the little things tells God we know that everything we have comes from Him and we are willing to trust Him to provide what He thinks we need for any given day.

I'm grateful for my coffee maker for that morning. God used the sight of it to reverse the negativity of the night and turn my day into songs of joy. He reminded me that He is good and He controls all that happens. Because of His best intentions for me, I can ask for His help in navigating through the rest of my day.

What anxious thoughts parade through your night? Do the next thing, that thing you always do immediately each morning. As you flow into the routine of your day, take note of even the small things you have and whatever brings you pleasure. They're all gifts from God, everyday reminders that He's taking care of you. He has given you all that you need, and He is working to bring you through the tough moments.

GRATITUDE PROMPT

What sights and sounds greet you first thing in the morning? Make a list. Thank God for each one. Tell God you'll keep trusting Him to show His unfailing love for you.

9

Books

Jesus did many other things as well. If every one of them
were written down, I suppose that even the whole world
would not have room for the books that would be written.

JOHN 21:25

To say I loved to read when I was a child is an understatement.
That's what my family would tell you.

Truth? I was obsessed.

I was the kid who hid behind the couch so Grandma couldn't
catch me and find a job for me to do. In fifth grade, I set the
lofty goal of reading all the fiction books in our school library by
author in alphabetical order. (I made it slightly past Louisa May
Alcott's *Little Women*.) To my family's consternation, I could sit
in a family gathering with a book pressed against my face, con-
tribute to the conversation, and still give a detailed account of
the last few pages I'd read. Poor vision didn't stop me. I would
read myself into massive headaches because, well, I liked to read.

I could not imagine a world without books. Books should be
an essential part of home décor, right? Doesn't every home own
at least one bookshelf that lures visitors to check out titles and
launch into a litany of their favorite reads?

It took me years to discover that owning even one book is a
privilege.

Imagine the books you own arranged neatly on a row of bookshelves. Mentally add the books available to you on the internet. Now consider a society with no written language. For the record, over three thousand languages—almost half the world's current living languages—don't even have an alphabet. That also means no reading primers, no literacy, and therefore no books. Bookshelves would be a useless piece of furniture.

Granted, it's more complex than that. People without a written native language may know how to read in another tongue—but it's not as comfortable. Many ethnic groups may have a written language, but most people don't know how to read. Factor in the statistic of those whose limited eyesight prohibits them from reading. So if you own books, can see to read, have the education to know how to read, your spoken words have been formed into written letters, and your economy is substantial enough to produce printed material, you are rich indeed.

What's important about books?

Books educate, inform, encourage, and entertain. They record the story of an indigenous people: their history, their successes and struggles, their mistakes and mindsets. Books profile lives of individuals who have made a difference in that society and provide an escape clause when daily demands and current crises threaten to defeat the readers. Books tell of the past so we don't make the same mistakes in the future. And books stretch our minds and knowledge banks to discover how to do daily tasks differently, explore worlds beyond our own, and look at life from a different perspective.

And then there's the best book of all. What would our faith walk be without the written context of the Bible? God's Word records the centuries-long, sweeping account of His plan to bring the wayward human race back to himself. If we relied solely on oral tradition, doctrine and stories of our faith would eventually drift into an uninformed and misinformed faith. The written word preserves the accuracy of our beliefs.

As the enduring message of God, the Bible contains instant

access to reminders of who God is, what He has done, and what He plans for the future. It gives clear direction about how to trust and obey this God who wants to have a close personal relationship with us. We can read for ourselves the beautiful account of the life and message of Jesus.

Further, when our emotions threaten to overthrow our memories, reading words of encouragement found in the Bible helps our faith find solid ground. No wonder a discouraged, lonely prisoner named Paul said to his protégé, Timothy, "When you come, bring the cloak that I left with Carpus at Troas, and my scrolls, especially the parchments" (2 Timothy 4:13). The apostle Paul missed the written word of God.

Nevertheless, homes throughout the world have no Bibles. While those who speak English have more translation options than any other language, many language groups have only one or two translation choices, and those may be inadequate or outdated.

When life gets tough, we can pick up our Bibles and discover how we can make it through our hard moments. Merely picking up a book can be a gratitude check, for we have books, and we can read.

How can we show active thanks to God for books? Here are some ideas:

- Make wise choices of the books you read.
- Thank God for the book you hold before you open its cover.
- Pass forward the blessing of reading material to other people.
- Support ministries involved in Bible translation or Bible literacy.

As we realize that we have what many do not have, let's determine to love and treasure books (especially God's Word) even more.

GRATITUDE PROMPT

Thank God for the gifts of written language, printed books, and the Bible. Ask God to guide your reading choices and for His suggestion of a person you can bless with a book.

10

Music

I will give thanks to the LORD because of his righteousness;
I will sing the praises of the name of the LORD Most High.

PSALM 7:17

One of my favorite recordings is Mendelssohn's *Italian Symphony*, as featured in the 1979 movie *Breaking Away*. I have to admit that I'm partially swayed because of how much I enjoy the movie. The inspiring story tells about Dave, a wannabe cyclist who, during his coming-of-age, loved all things Italian. Mendelssohn's cheerful, bouncing composition is the perfect backdrop. Whenever I hear the motifs of the *Italian Symphony*, I envision Dave's bicycle streaming through traffic on its trek to victory. You can almost hear the pedals turning to the beat of the fast-paced music. You feel like pulling the camera of your mind into a bird's-eye view of the landscape, looking ahead for the bicycle's final destination. And all the while, with each wheel rotation, you excitedly vocalize the momentum—*forward, forward.*

Music's rhythm, melody, and harmony give an added breadth and depth to our thoughts and words. With music we express one thought in myriads of ways. We have Jubal to thank for the invention of music. Seven generations down from Adam through Cain, the Bible says Jubal was the father of all who play stringed instruments and pipes (Genesis 4:21). Yet music existed earlier, for God put songs in the throats of birds on the fifth day of creation. The place of music in God's world took flight, and we've all been enriched ever since.

I love music.

I love making music and listening to it. Music allows us to express our emotions in healthy ways. It enhances our worship of God when mere spoken words seem inadequate. I'm not a composer and I limit my performances anymore to the walls of my own home, but music still feeds my creative hunger, allowing me to express my deepest longings and greatest joys with creative ingenuity.

Like anything, music can be used for good or for evil and selfish means. We can praise God with joyful sounds, or we can promote ungodly ideas and destructive emotions. We can inspire or we can incite. We can sing sad songs, passing our grievances to the hearts of others, or we can use song to convey praise to God, boosting our own spirits and brightening the day of those around us.

God calls us to use His gift of music in our praise to Him. The word *sing* appears sixty-nine times in the book of Psalms alone. God encourages His people to create original songs (Psalm 96:1), use a variety of instruments (Psalm 150), and both sing and shout for joy (98:4) in their worship of Him. The psalmists suggest praise prompts: sing because of God's righteousness (7:17), strength (59:16), love (89:1), and His justice (101:1).

If you aren't a music lover, the psalmist doesn't let you off the hook. Check out the last verse of Psalm 150: "Let everything that has breath praise the Lord" (v. 6). The verse doesn't say, "If you can carry a tune," "If you can read music," or "If you've had formal music training." If you have breath—and we all do—then God includes you in His invitation to join His praise band, even if it is engaging with the message of the song within the silence of your thoughts. But please do try to sing along. God loves a joyful noise—*any* joyful noise—that comes from a sincere heart.

Music is God's reciprocal gift. God created music and then gave it to us. We use it to praise Him. God also longs to help us grow closer to Him. He reminds us of His words and ways through prompting of the Holy Spirit. The best way for God to catch our attention might be through a song's melody.

In fact, music is a wonderful mnemonic device. I remember Bible verses much better when they are set to music. Much like Mendelssohn's *Italian Symphony* reminds me of bicycle wheels and pushing on to victory, certain melodies have forever entrenched reassuring Bible phrases into my brain and heart. Melodies wrapped around Scriptures like "My peace I give you" (John 14:27) and "You are my hiding place" (Psalm 32:7) travel with me throughout my day to reassure me of who God is and what He has done. They reinforce that God is in charge, He loves me, and He knows all that is happening to me.

Melody combined with Bible-based words can act like the soft touch of a hug, a gentle voice of peace, and a healing salve spread upon our souls. One friend tells how music has been a lifeline in some of her darkest moments and how the right song would come on the radio at just the right time. Another friend compares her favorite traditional hymns to a "warm bowl of homemade chicken noodle soup on a cold, dreary winter day."

See how notes fill the space between our hearts and His ears? The duet of melody and words lifts our spirits, blossoming hope into more vibrant praise, and the cycle begins again. It's the gift that keeps on giving.

How is your day going? If it's going well, sing songs of praise. If troubles threaten to pull you down, pray for God's deliverance (James 5:13). Then find a song to sing, even if it is merely under your breath, thanking God for the gift of music that empowers you to center your heart and emotions on Him.

Don't wait till a worship service on Sunday. Now is the time to sing.

GRATITUDE PROMPT

What praise song has run through your mind recently? Sing, hum, find a soundtrack, play the melody on your favorite instrument, or internalize the tune in your mind. Thank God for the gift of music that lets you express your love for Him and reminds you how much He loves you.

11

Time

He has made everything beautiful in its time. He has
also set eternity in the human heart; yet no one can
fathom what God has done from beginning to end.

ECCLESIASTES 3:11

Time. It's a flat-rate gift. Everyone gets an equal amount—
twenty-four hours per day. It's ours to manage its use.

That's where I have a problem. I confess. I don't like what I
call "wasting time." Something drives me to make every moment
count. Perhaps that stems from my childhood upbringing. We
were taught to stay busy, that work was a good thing. And as I
age, I find I want to be as productive as possible before I lose
more vision and overall health. Maybe you identify with me in
sensing the tick of our life clock growing louder the older we get.

For years, whenever I read Proverbs 16:3—"Commit to the
LORD whatever you do"—I inwardly argued that I had to do my
part regardless of what God seemed to be doing or whoever might
be "distracting" me from my preconceived task list. Frustration
brewed when someone else's time mismanagement hampered my
efforts to make the most of each moment. I had not yet realized
that time was a part of God's creation as much as anything else.

I could relax in gratitude and trust that He was in charge of what happened with each hour of my life, not me.

Let's start at the beginning. The author of Genesis documented the first day of creation by saying, "There was evening, and there was morning—the first day" (Genesis 1:5). On the fourth day of creation, God put markers in the sky—the sun and moon—to help people track the passage of time (Genesis 1:14). Since we're finite beings, we need distinct markers that remind us when to rest and wake.

But God's plan included more than numbers on a clock face. As part of our human makeup, God inserted an eternity chip into our hearts (see Ecclesiastes 3:11). Our human brains might struggle to comprehend how God could exist before the beginning of creation. Yet our sense of past and future empowers us to begin to grasp God's ability to see all of time all at once.

Moreover, if God designed the ticking clock, He is in control of it. And His rule over creation means He has the power and authority to alter any part of it as He sees best. That includes the dimension of time. The Israelite leader, Joshua, and his army were running out of daylight, jeopardizing the victory of a crucial battle. Joshua prayed that the sun and moon would stand still. And it did—not for a few moments or a few hours but for an entire day (Joshua 10:12–14). Can you imagine all that had to transpire in the solar system for that to happen? God could do that—because He is God.

What does God's management of the clock mean for you and me? We don't have to worry about running out of time to accomplish God's tasks for us. He knows our future and He is in control of all that happens in the past, present, and future.

That's a game changer for how I manage my day.

Am I running late to an appointment and traffic is heavy? Relax! God is in control. He'll take care of the details. If events don't happen as I anticipate or expect, I can trust that His agenda will bring honor to His name.

If a friend stops by and the conversation turns to spiritual matters, I need not worry that I'm not marking off tasks. Instead, I can accept that God has rearranged my priorities for the day. After all, eternal matters are more important, with further-reaching impact than getting my house clean.

If my family oversleeps, pushing my planned-to-the-moment schedule off kilter, I can ask God, "How would you like me to use this unexpected, unplanned block of time?" Perhaps God has orchestrated that quiet hour so I can spend time praying for my sleeping family, the day's events, or other matters the Lord brings to my mind. Instead of fretting, I can thank Him for giving me extra moments with Him.

If our day starts with thanks for the gift of time, imagine how that can alter our stress levels about getting everything done. Our gratitude accepts that moments come from God and He is ultimately in control of our schedule, not us. The rest of Proverbs 16:3 says, "and he will establish your plans." When we submit our agenda to God, thanking Him for being in control, He will give us all the time we need to accomplish His most important tasks.

GRATITUDE PROMPT

Thank God for the way He constructed His gift of time and that He is in control of your hours. Entrust the rest of your day to Him, thanking Him that He knows all that will happen and that it will be the best plan for both Him and you.

PART TWO

Looking at Life from Another Angle

As the heavens are higher than the earth,
so are my ways higher than your ways
and my thoughts than your thoughts.

ISAIAH 55:9

The world wants to identify and label what we consider blessings. Godly gratitude looks at life from God's vantage point.

12

Aquariums

How many are your works, Lord!
In wisdom you made them all;
the earth is full of your creatures.
Psalm 104:24

As my husband paid the bill for my birthday dinner, I wandered into the restaurant's empty foyer and discovered a large fish tank filled with tropical fish. When Jack joined me, I pointed to the aquarium.

Rather than being entranced by the contents of such a large tank in a Southern Arizona restaurant where I could stand nose to nose with the brightly colored fish, I blurted a rather ungrateful, "I so wish we'd visited Shedd Aquarium when we lived in Illinois."

My desire was real and long entrenched. Having grown up in the Southwest desert, I saw ocean life as exotic and fascinating. Before my better-than-ever surgery, a disastrous visit to the Columbus Zoo and Aquarium, where crowds and a cranky docent kept me from getting close enough to see the sea life in the tank, left me craving another chance. When we moved to Illinois, the famed Shedd Aquarium was a delightful three-hour train ride from our home. But in ten years of living there, we never went. A dream unfulfilled. Now we lived once again in the Southwest, and my dream dried up as fast as monsoon moisture on a hot summer day.

Yet here was a fish tank. No one else was in the restaurant foyer. My loving heavenly Father held out an exclusive invitation for me to enjoy what I had always wanted to see, up close, no less. With a bit of embarrassment and a bit more remorse, I chose to embrace gratitude for what was before me rather than pining for what I had left behind.

Our human brains are experts at linking present experiences to past memories and desires. And Satan is a master at luring us into ingratitude by whispering in our ear, "Remember what you could have had?"

The nation of Israel had that problem. We see it in Numbers 11:1–8.

Manna was a kind of grain God miraculously sprinkled on the desert ground to feed the Israelites. Anything tastes good when you're hungry. But after months of manna, the novelty wore off. The people had a case of selective memory. They remembered the good food of Egypt: the fish, cucumbers, leeks, and melons. Somehow they forgot the very real brutality of their past slavery. They discounted the glory of the Lord that resided with them every day. And they ignored the miracle of manna, a gift that appeared morning after morning without fail from a merciful God.

God had done all kinds of fantastic, incredible miracles for them that generations after them would remember and praise, and all they could think about were fish and cucumbers.

Back in the restaurant, I peered closer at the fish tank and whispered an apology to my Lord God. He had poured life into sea creatures, whether they lived in a nationally known aquarium, the depths of the ocean, or a simple fish tank in the Desert Southwest. Their design was beautiful, colorful, intricate, and complex. Desert dwellers not so many generations before me never had the chance to see tropical fish. I and anyone else living in landlocked locations are privileged that we get to see them at all.

When we pine for the past and long for lost opportunities, we show a careless disregard for the gifts God puts within our present moments. The tropical fish breathed a Thank You! prompt to me. The next time the words "I wish I could have" form in my mouth, I need to mold those words into thanks for what I have in front of me.

Look around your day. What gifts has God given you? Turn Satan's weapon of selective memory against him. Use the link of the past to ricochet to the present and thank God for what you have today.

GRATITUDE PROMPT

Write down five blessings God has given to you today, and post them in a place you can see them often. How are these blessings better than what you have had in your past?

13

Pots and Pans

I have learned the secret of being content in any
and every situation, whether well fed or hungry,
whether living in plenty or in want.

PHILIPPIANS 4:12

I walked into my daughter's kitchen. "See what I got for Christmas?" she said as her hand gestured toward her stove. There sat a new set of T-Fal cookware.

Matching her smile took effort. I wanted new cookware. By comparison, my thirty-six-year-marriage-old Revere Ware looked, well, old. Used. If lots of wear means lots of love, like the tale of *The Velveteen Rabbit* suggests, my cookware had an adoring family. My thoughts became tinged with jealousy. Why can't I afford nice new things like her? How long has she been married? Only three years?

Jealousy is such a joy sucker.

The Old Testament king Ahab discovered the problem with jealousy the hard way. We see the story in 1 Kings 21. His neighbor, Naboth, held family property, a vineyard, next door to the royal palace. Ahab wanted Naboth's property. It would be convenient to have a vegetable garden right outside his back door. But when he offered his neighbor a generous settlement, Naboth said no.

Under Old Testament law, the land was not his to sell; it had to stay in the family.

Ahab did not take that refusal well. As king, he deserved the conveniences of life, right? Ahab's desire grew into discontent which festered into full-blown resentment and retaliation. Trumping up false charges against Naboth, Ahab had his neighbor executed and claimed the vineyard for his own.

Most of us have not resorted to murder to get what we want. Yet desire for what others have can sap life out of relationships and blur the happiness of our own everyday moments. And like many things, discontent is not as straight a line as, "You have what I want, and I'm not happy about it."

We see the neighbor's lavish Christmas display and then look at our one string of lights, wondering if we're celebrating Christmas properly. Or we watch the other grandma spoil the grandkids with gifts. Knowing we can't afford to do the same, we fret we might be seen as inferior grandparents. Unfortunately, the moment we start making comparisons, we lose perspective. Desire mushes into dissatisfaction.

The apostle Paul learned through his own set of life experiences that contentment in all circumstances is possible. While thanking the Philippian church for their generous gift, he reflected on his own attitude toward possessions. If Paul had the extras, great. If he didn't, that was okay too.

How do we move from Ahab's irritation to Paul's serenity? How do we find grateful contentment for what we have even when we are surrounded by others who have more?

Remember how you got what you have. My daughter told me she received the set of cookware from her in-laws as a Christmas present. Then I remembered. My husband's parents, hearing I liked to cook, gave us our Revere Ware the Christmas before we were married. Talk about confidence that we'd go through with the wedding! My daughter and I were both blessed with quality cookware from loving in-laws.

Remember what you want most. Knowing quality and durability were important to me, my in-laws intentionally selected a set that would last throughout our married life. And it has. It's still perfectly good cookware, even after decades of loving use. What a blessing to have reliable cookware so I don't have to spend money for a new set.

Remember the benefits of what you have. As I look at my daughter's cookware today, I wonder what appealed to me when I first saw it. Her set requires special utensils and should never go in the dishwasher. Me? No restraints, no problem! Looking at the benefits flipped my momentary greed back to gratitude.

Paul challenges us to claim a mindset of consistent contentment. Accepting that everything is a gift from God brings us the level of satisfaction Paul experienced. We can trust that God will make sure we have whatever we need to honor and serve Him at the proper moment. If your cupboards are stuffed with pots and pans, enjoy the pleasure of the extra and use it to bless God's people through your culinary skill. But hold it loosely, realizing God will help you get along without it if necessary. If all you have is a single aluminum pot, God can give you the creativity to find ways to bless others and honor Him with your one pot, and you will find that it is enough.

Jealousy is a red flag of our need for a gratitude adjustment, and gratitude is an anecdote for keeping jealousy at bay. Yet jealousy and discontent creep in at unsuspecting moments when we're weak, tired, and unsatisfied with other parts of life. We can blur our jealous thoughts into the background by focusing on what we do have and why we have it. Recounting the qualities and benefits of what we already have gives us the confidence we need to tell temptation, "What I have is enough. It's just right. It's exactly what God wants me to have."

And gratitude overflows when we find out later just how right God's provision was.

GRATITUDE PROMPT

What areas of life tempt you to be discontent? If the possessions of others highlight your lack, write down what you already have and how God provided it for you. Thank God for all His good gifts.

14

Rainy Days

He covers the sky with clouds;
he supplies the earth with rain
and makes grass grow on the hills.

Psalm 147:8

"Don't you *love* this weather we're having?" The postal clerk's voice dripped with sarcasm as she took my money for my purchase.

"Oh, I'm willing to put up with it." I smiled at her. "It's been dry for so long, I'm sure the farmers appreciate it."

She was not smiling. "It can rain at night, then," she said. "Not during the day when I've got plans."

My smile turned into a grin. "It gives me a good excuse to stay inside and read a book."

She leaned over the counter. "You're determined to be positive about this rainy weather, aren't you?"

I slung my purse over my shoulder. "Yeah. I am."

We had a saying in the farming community where I lived at the time that there's no such thing as a happy farmer. Either there's not enough rain or it rained too much. Worse yet, too much too fast.

"What would make you happy?" I asked one farmer. He had

it all worked out. "An inch a week during growing season; a slow, steady rain and no hail."

Alas, life isn't that simple or predictable. I find it ironic that wherever I've lived, many local people are like my farmer friends. Rainfall is either too much or not enough, and it's always at the wrong time. And then there are those days when unexpected moments fall like a sudden cloudburst. Too much goes wrong in a compacted space of time. Interruptions happen at the least convenient moment. Winds of change scatter my well-formed plans faster than a two-minute microburst. And tedium and tiredness slow my momentum, draping a canopy of emotional clouds over everything I attempt to accomplish.

How can I be thankful when rain or any out-of-my-control event dampens my plans, messes with my mood, or worse yet, ruins a year's worth of planning, planting, and nurturing, like a farmer losing an entire corn crop from one hailstorm?

As creator of the wet stuff, God himself put weather patterns in place. He created both rainfall and drought. Snow and fog. Hurricanes? Part of the system. Tornadoes? Those too.

Do I understand why all of these are part of His creation? No, I don't.

And as cyclical as weather is, to add another wrinkle to our understanding, Scripture tells of times when God specifically directed a weather event. Remember when Noah built the ark because God warned him of a whole earth flood? Or the time Moses delivered a message from God to Pharaoh telling the leader to let the Israelites go or "I will send the worst hailstorm that has ever fallen on Egypt" (Exodus 9:17)? Pharaoh didn't, so God did. And don't forget the story in 1 Kings 17 of Elijah announcing, in the Lord's name, a three-year drought—and boy did things get dry.

As humans, we don't know why God directs weather or any other act of nature or history as He does. Our ignorance leads us to inaccurate conclusions that question God's choices. Our heads accept His creation and the cycles He has set in motion. But we have only fragmented clues. So, when we grumble about the rain, the sun, the darkness, the unexpected—the timing or amount—we, in our incomplete knowledge, are contesting God's wisdom, goodness, and greater purposes.

But sometimes rain does mess up our plans. In big ways. How could a good and wise God allow things such as flooded basements and ruined crops?

Gratitude accepts God's all-knowing, all-encompassing wisdom. Gratitude admits that in my human frailty and tendency toward self-focus, I don't know or understand everything. God calls us to thank Him for the rain and sun equally, for He is Creator-God, and He has a purpose for whatever He created. He calls us to make redemptive use of the messed-up moments and find contentment in the rearrangement of our schedules, remembering that He oversees all our plans anyway.

Isaiah's words have soothed my personal angst many times:

> As the rain and the snow
>   come down from heaven,
> and do not return to it
>   without watering the earth
> and making it bud and flourish,
>   so that it yields seed for the sower and bread
>   for the eater,
> so is my word that goes out from my mouth:
>   It will not return to me empty,
> but will accomplish what I desire
>   and achieve the purpose for which I sent it.
>   (Isaiah 55:10–11)

Viewing the weather as a gift from God and choosing to rest in God's direction of earth's rhythms that rainy day, I left the post office, went home, and read a book. And the clerk? Every time after that encounter, she greeted me with a warm smile and positive comments. I'm not sure whether she was merely having a bad day that one time, she was now afraid to be grumpy in front of me, or my contentment changed her outlook.

Whatever the case, our conversation taught me that gratitude doesn't have to be forced. When we internalize the truth that all of creation is a gift from God, even when nature's rhythms clash with our personal plans, thankfulness becomes a mindset and flows naturally from us.

And others notice.

GRATITUDE PROMPT

Thank God for His beautifully created gift of weather in all its various forms. Thank Him for His guidance in managing your life activities when rain causes complications in your day.

15

Time Change

You are my strength,
I sing praise to you;
you, God, are my fortress,
my God on whom I can rely.

PSALM 59:17

Most folks think I am bound and determined to be positive about rainy days. I'd lose my reputation for sunshiny outlooks if they knew how I feel about daylight saving time.

I must have an inflexible bio-clock. I've never handled the semi-annual time shift well. My body doesn't respond like everyone says it will. Gaining an extra hour in the fall makes me feel exhausted by day's end. No wonder God created a twenty-four-hour day. My body can't handle twenty-five. And spring forward? There's no spring in my step. I feel like a grumpy bear, awakened prematurely from its hibernation.

When we moved to Arizona, I breathed an initial sigh of relief. No more time changes. But my celebration was short lived. Arizonans have to track when the rest of the world messes with their clocks. We're constantly asking our back-East friends, "Are you two or three hours ahead of us—and when do you change again?" A year-round daylight saving time would solve the issue with twice-a-year biorhythm mess-ups, but the grumpier among us want to say, "Why can't you leave things the way God made them?"

Why? God invented time and left it up to people to find innovative ways to chronicle and manage it. God made people and time, and people made clocks. And considering we live in a fallen world where some of mankind's ideas are fantastic and others are real bloopers, those of us who aren't in charge of change get the task of learning to live with the ebb and flow of society's whims and ill-conceived ideas.

I still don't like it. I also don't like it when my own body rhythms and hormonal shifts throw off my sleep routines. But God calls me to be thankful in all circumstances. How can I possibly be grateful for any kind of time change? Can I sincerely thank God when the trash truck wakes me up an hour early and throws my whole day off kilter? When the neighbor's barking dog steals an hour of sleep at 2:00 a.m.? Or when I lie awake till midnight because I ate too much at a late supper, and then I oversleep and feel draggy the next day? Can I find gratitude while slugging through a major case of jet lag that, truth to tell, I didn't take the necessary steps to minimize?

God's power is made perfect in weakness, Paul said. For when I'm weak, I have the chance to tap into God's power and discover how strong I can be through Him (2 Corinthians 12:9–10). I often think of those verses in terms of the suffering Paul went through: the exhaustion he details in caring for the churches, preaching the gospel to hostile or ambivalent crowds, and traveling storm-torn seas. My fussing over interrupted sleep pales in comparison to his energy-sapping adventures. If God's strength is available in massive troubles, it's certainly also there for us on the days when we've lost several hours of sleep for whatever out-of-our-control reason.

God is consistent. He is the same yesterday, today, and forever (Hebrews 13:8). He has unlimited strength that is always at an even flow. And that strength is available to us no matter what happens during our day or night to disrupt our rhythms.

We just need to ask.

I started teaching a Sunday school class for early elementary kids when I was in college. The day came when I stayed out too late Saturday night and had barely prepared my lesson. I arrived at church bleary-eyed and foggy focused, ashamed to admit to my mentor-mother how ill prepared I was to teach.

Desperation is a great prayer motivator. In my panic, I begged God, "You've got to help me." Over the next hour, creative ideas and workarounds flowed through my mind. I felt incredible energy, and I could tell the kids were grasping the life application behind the lesson. I'm convinced I learned the most of anyone that day: when I am weak, tired, or sleep deprived, God's strength is available to me.

Psalm 59:17 says, "[God,] you are my strength, I sing praise to you; you, God, are my fortress, my God on whom I can rely." Isn't that wonderful? No matter how messed up our day or night might be, we do have enough energy to make it through because we can rely on God to fill us up, reorganize our priorities, lighten the next day's load, or teach us new lessons through the experience that will make us stronger for the next round. When we are weak, through His power, we are strong. That's worth thanking God for.

Any time shift in our lives invites us to gratefully trust God's capacity to give us what we need to meet for the moment. We can thank Him for His power that enables us to do what He calls us to do, despite the obstacles we face.

No matter what time it is.

GRATITUDE PROMPT

The next time your biorhythms get disrupted, ask God to reorient your priorities, and then thank Him for helping you make it through your day and for what He will accomplish through you despite your lack of energy.

16

Pimentos

Go and make disciples of all nations.
MATTHEW 28:19

I pride myself that I have only a short list of foods I absolutely will not eat. Pimentos is one of them. I don't even want to touch or cook with the slimy things.

Imagine my gut-level reaction when the kitchen director of the international Bible training center where I served as a two-week short-term worker handed me a jar of pimentos. "Would you slice these for the sandwiches we're making for lunch?" she asked. Why must I be the one to slice one of the three foods I absolutely will not eat? Or touch?

I was convinced I couldn't. I have done everything you've asked me to do in this kitchen, I thought. Please don't ask me to cut up pimentos.

But how could I say no? My silent response turned to a prayer: Oh God, you have got to help me get over my gag reflex. If you want me to cut up pimentos, I'll do it. But I am not happy.

Then I remembered what the kitchen director had said in our first training session. "You aren't peeling potatoes, making soup, or cooking a meal. You are training disciple makers to do kingdom work in their home countries."

I looked at the slimy red thing in my hand. Our group of American volunteers were cooking meals for this group of students so they could fully dedicate two weeks of their lives to studying the Bible and receiving ministry leadership training—without having to stop to cook and clean up. The students had sacrificed and confronted danger so they could come to this sanctuary place to hone their ministry skills and improve their Bible knowledge.

Pimentos were not the focus. The students were. So as I sliced, I began to thank God for the students in the classroom on the other side of the kitchen wall. I thanked God for their courage and passion and for calling each of them to evangelize and encourage the people in their own countries. Before I knew it, the pimentos lay in a neat pile, and I had forgotten how slimy they felt.

All of us have lists of personal preferences: food favorites, color choices, music styles, or organizational structure. Whenever we work with a group of people, part of team unity is learning to compromise and relinquish personal inclinations for the good of the group's goals. But oh, it can be hard. Especially when one person has strong feelings. It's so easy and tempting to magnify what we want and make that the main issue.

God calls us to look at the bigger picture of His kingdom work.

Liking something is not a requirement for gratitude. We can still thank God for something even if it is not our personal preference. Gratitude will overshadow our personal tastes when we step back and see our work as part of God's overarching plan.

I may not like pimentos. You might not care for the music ministry's use of high-definition TV screens or a particular aspect of a volunteer job you've been asked to do. It's all right for us to dislike those things. God has made each of us uniquely different, complete with our own suitcase of preferences and aversions. We can still thank God for those less desirable things. Other people do like them, and they can be a tiny but useful tool in training disciple makers for God's kingdom work.

We can also thank God for the personal lesson of humility.

Cutting up pimentos challenged me to set myself aside so I could serve others. In doing so, I followed the example of Jesus, who said that "the Son of Man did not come to be served, but to serve, and to give his life as a ransom for many" (Matthew 20:28).

What is something you don't care for? Have you wished you didn't have to deal with that thing? Flip your personal dislikes and examine how God is using or could use what you don't like for His glory. God will use anything in His creation to accomplish His purposes. If what we personally dislike effectively speaks to the hearts and minds of people who need to draw closer to Him, it's worth our words of gratitude.

When we appreciate how God has chosen to use us in the greater work of telling the world about Jesus, we'll have far fewer objections to the things we once found distasteful. Even pimentos.

GRATITUDE PROMPT

Think of something you don't particularly like or that is not your preference, whether a food, music style, or daily task. Thank God for that one thing and ask Him to show you how it blesses others.

17

Delays

I will sing the LORD's praise, for he has been good to me.

PSALM 13:6

The line leading to customs at the Dulles International Airport stretched across a massive waiting area, up two sets of escalators, and out of sight. Our nine-hour international flight from Europe, where my aunt and I had spent two weeks on a mission trip, was delayed in landing, giving us barely two hours to make it through customs and to our next gate on the other side of the airport. Not used to the timetables of international travel, I looked at my watch for about the tenth time. My aunt, a seasoned traveler, reached out her hand as if to cover my wristwatch. "Let go of that next departure time," she said. "It's the airline's job to get you home. If we miss the next flight, they'll take care of us."

Calendar apps and alarm reminders can be wonderful things, but they do us a disservice in placing an indelible time stamp on our brains. They're great if everything goes according to plan. But I've learned that a specific time for any life event is like a weather forecast. None of us can predict the future. None of us can override what might mess up our plans at any given time.

Perhaps that's why we don't like delays. They reveal that we're not in control.

Before the era of smart phones or even wristwatches, Saul, the first king of Israel, had trouble accepting a delay. 1 Samuel 13 tells how the prophet Samuel told Saul to wait seven days for Samuel to join him at Gilgal. So the king spent his hours assembling his troops to fight against the Philistines, but Samuel didn't show up. Saul's troops started to scatter, and Saul tired of the delay. The king took matters into his own hands and, wrongfully taking the role of a priest, made a burnt offering to seek God's favor before going into battle.

Then Samuel arrived. An *unhappy* Samuel arrived.

Saul paid a heavy price for his impatience with the delay which led him to disobey God's command. The kingdom would not pass to his sons, Samuel told him, but to David, a man after God's own heart.

David had issues with delays too, but in Psalm 13, he shows a better way to handle them. He admitted his angst to the Lord, for he cried out, "How long, LORD? Will you forget me forever?" (v. 1). David poured out his frustration, anxiety, and sorrow at the wait. But then the psalm records this thought: "I trust in your unfailing love; my heart rejoices in your salvation. I will sing the LORD's praise, for he has been good to me" (vv. 5–6).

How could David say that? Is he being dishonest or flippant?

No. David simply knew who was in control. He accepted that it was God's job, not his, to get him where he needed to be. David's past encounters with God had proved to him that God is not a procrastinator. A delay is not God's denial to do what we need Him to do. What seems like postponements and snags from our vantage point are merely footholds to bring us to God's bigger plan. He will keep His promises to us. Our part of the contract is to accept that the hands of His clock may not necessarily match up with the rigidity of our smartphone alarms.

At the airport, I couldn't see beyond the escalator to know the frenetic activity happening at customs to process travelers so they could catch their flights on time. In the same way, I cannot see beyond the mountain I'm currently climbing to know what God is doing on my behalf. In God's schedule, what is important is not so much how soon His plan gets done but that it does get done at the right time.

Once again, trust and gratitude link arms. You and I can thank God for delays because we trust His plan and time frames. If we look at the clock, we'll be constantly disappointed, and we'll feel like God has failed us. But when we relinquish our plans to Him, realizing He does not disclose exact times for any of His great works (including the time of His Son's return to earth), we will find that God is good, loving, and faithful. Every single time. And we discover that what seemed like a delay was exactly on schedule according to His agenda.

Gratitude produces peace and contentment. As my aunt and I reached the escalators, we witnessed several impatient travelers, stewing vocally about the delay. My aunt grinned at me. "They're not having a good day, are they?" But we were. Because we chose to let God oversee our trip home, we were at peace. And peace is preferable to anxiety, which doesn't feel so good when you're already tired from a nine-hour flight, a nine-month troubled pregnancy, or a nine-year wait for that job you've waited and worked hard for.

As I reached home after that international flight at exactly the time my ticket said I would, I came to another crucial realization. I'm glad God manages life events. The simple truth is this: I couldn't do any better. Not by a long shot.

GRATITUDE PROMPT

The next time a delay comes into your life, thank God that He is the one who is ultimately in control.

18

Shopping Trips

Seek first his kingdom and his righteousness, and
all these things will be given to you as well.

MATTHEW 6:33

S atisfaction guaranteed.
Many businesses make that claim or your money back.
The business is saying they're willing to stand behind the quality
of their product.

Businesspeople, I have a secret to tell you.

My satisfaction is up to me as much as it is up to you. *Shh.*

Here's what I mean. If my happiness is based on finding everything on my shopping list at the price and quality I want in less
than half an hour, I'm bound to be disappointed. But if I invite
God to be part of my store experience and look at my shopping
trip from His vantage point, wonderful things can happen that
will plaster a smile on my face, free of charge.

My husband and I received the gift of empty hands and full
hearts one lovely fall evening. We had gone to our local Walmart
for three items. We struck out on all three. But when I asked an
employee about the location of sugar-free whipped topping, he
left his stack of boxes to show me where I could find it. When

he didn't find it there, he went the extra mile—okay, two extra rows—to look another place. He was so kind!

Then when my husband headed his electric cart toward the exit, a limping woman approached us. "Oh, please, are you done with your cart?" We gladly relinquished it, joking that now we didn't have to put it away. I don't know if she was praying for a cart, but if she was, we were the answer to her prayer.

Another shopping trip, I spoke to a little girl who clutched a stuffed animal to her chest. I pointed to what I thought was a bear but was quickly corrected. Not hearing what she said, I tried to recover. "What's its name?"

"It doesn't have a name."

"What?" Enter drama queen grandma. "Everybody needs a name."

Two aisles later, she approached me. "I have a name! It's Bella."

"Great name," I said. "Better than the name I came up with."

"What was that?"

"Sonya. But I like Bella better."

I saw my new little friend at the checkout, and her mother turned to me. "Thank you for talking with my daughter," she said.

Relief. I hadn't come across as some weird stranger.

I don't remember what I bought that day. But I do remember the smile of a little girl hugging her stuffed whatever-it-was.

We all have to-do lists. But Jesus invites us to make life more than the daily drudge of getting stuff done. His kingdom calls us to represent His life wherever we go.

It's part of what we call the Great Commission found in Matthew 28:19–20. Jesus's first word is "Go." But the Greek for the word *go* is not a command. The verse should be translated, "As you go, make disciples." Wherever we are, whatever we're doing, we take the gospel with us. We live it, speak it, and represent it in everything we do.

That means that shopping trips take on the dual function of relational opportunities with eternal implications. And that can make a mediocre shopping trip more exciting than a trip to Disneyland.

That lovely fall evening experience at Walmart taught me to invite the Lord to go with me into the craziness of the Christmas shopping season. I started to pray before entering a store, "Lord, use me to be a blessing to someone." That season, I intentionally engaged clerks in conversation, asked how they were, and showed sympathy for their aching feet. I never found out what they thought about my overtures of compassion, but I do know my stress level plummeted. Other customers probably wondered how I could possibly be happy about Christmas shopping. My joy came from partnering with God to make my shopping trips about the people as much as about my list.

In Matthew 6:33, Jesus said, "Seek first his kingdom and his righteousness, and all these things will be given to you as well." How do we put God's kingdom first? Imagine this: What would happen if all of us who are reading these words thanked God for letting us come to a particular store on our next shopping trip and then surrendered our personal agenda to Him, asking, "Whom would You like me to bless today?" The potential for the spread of the good news of God's grace and love is downright exciting.

Shopping trips are only the beginning. We can partner with God on walks, in the workplace, and even in church functions as we set aside our own agendas and look for ways to be a blessing to others. We'll leave with a heart full of gratitude, for we will see God at work within us and through us in ways we could not have planned ourselves.

Satisfaction guaranteed.

GRATITUDE PROMPT

What's the next event on your calendar? Thank God for His delight in using you to represent Him wherever you go. Ask Him to use you to be a blessing to someone during that event.

19

Breakfast

He makes grass grow for the cattle, and plants for people
to cultivate—bringing forth food from the earth.
PSALM 104:14

When I was a junior in high school, my stepfather had to quit
work due to health issues. As we waited for his disability
benefits to start, we lived on savings, and my parents pinched
pennies till they squealed in protest. We rarely drove unless we
had to, and I learned to take the bus or walk where I needed
to go. My mother could make one whole chicken stretch over
three meals. Any grocery purchase was a calculated expenditure
involving higher math and compounded sales.

I remember the day my mother found a sale on bananas.
When she brought that fruit home, you would think we'd been
handed a platter of steak and lobster. At our next meal we savored
every bite. They tasted extra good, probably because we now saw
bananas as a special treat, not something common that we got
every day. Bananas now carried a higher value.

More value than I realized at the time. Because bananas are
readily available in retail grocery stores, we don't stop to think
about the hundreds of years it took to domesticate and cultivate
the common banana. And we certainly don't contemplate the

thousands of miles those bunches of fruit travel from the tropics to our North American tables. After a nine-month growing season, bananas travel by ship from Central America through the Panama Canal and land at store facilities, ready to be ripened by ethylene gas before arriving in stores. That banana you hold in your hand has been on a long, wearisome journey.

Bacon, another item on my breakfast table, may not travel as many miles but has been literally pounded and squished into the final shape I see on my plate. Our ancestors of a few generations back would slaughter their own pigs and cure the meat. Today we merely go to the store to bring home the bacon. But from pig to table, many unseen hands put the pork bellies through a skinning, curing, cooking, and refrigeration process before slicing, packaging, and sending the bacon to the stores.

When I was a little girl, I had a Bible story book that had one story I read many times. A little boy thanked his mother for his good bread. She said, "Don't thank me, thank the grocery man." So the boy did.

But the grocer said, "Don't thank me. Thank the farmer." And the little boy did. "Thank you for my good bread." Skipping to the end of the story, the sun and rain told the boy to thank God for his bread. And he did.

We take much for granted. It's all too easy to not think about the origin of a food beyond the food market. Yes, our heads know it comes from somewhere, but until we see a video on YouTube or TLC, we don't think through how fortunate we are to have bacon and bananas. We accept those things as part of everyday life—until the food market shelves are empty, the price goes up, or our paycheck dwindles. Then we notice.

As I rise to clear my breakfast dishes, I look around my house and realize just how much of what I have came through the hard work of countless generations. It's taken time and ingenuity to develop the processes that make my dishes, furniture, house wiring, and plumbing. Each food I eat is processed and packaged, and it pays somebody a living wage. I am truly blessed. If I had to make everything I own, like my ancestors did, I would have little time for anything else.

Imagine what they would think about our grocery stores. They would think it a miracle. And they might very well be right.

Ultimately, like the boy in my storybook discovered, everything we have comes from God. The Lord is the one who made the pigs and placed the wheat and banana seeds on the earth. He gave humans the knowledge and resourcefulness to discover how to process those raw resources into usable forms, like developing the cultivation of seedless bananas.

Now, when we bow our heads over our breakfast table, maybe we can find far more to thank God for than a generalized, "Thank you for my food." Our bacon and toast would grow cold and our banana turn spotty brown before we could finish the list of gratitude points for grocer, grower, cultivator, ships and stores, sunshine and rain, and God, the originator of it all. The emotion and sincerity of our gratitude will gain new depth when we pause to ponder what it took for the Lord to bring that meal to us.

Or, when our hearts are too full for words, we can fold our gratitude into one simple sentence: "Thank you, God, for all you created that made this meal possible for us. You are so good."

GRATITUDE PROMPT

At your next meal, thank God for each item on your plate. Thank Him for the people and process it took for that food to be there.

20

Brownies and Brussels Sprouts

Every good and perfect gift is from above, coming
down from the Father of the heavenly lights,
who does not change like shifting shadows.

JAMES 1:17

The little local church my family attended when I was a
teenager was the center of my existence. I went to every
event: revivals, fellowship meals, youth group fundraisers, and
impromptu parties. You name it, I was there. The church became
my social support system, my family. I loved those dear people.

I quickly noticed two things about church functions outside
of worship services. First, there was usually food. Second, we
always prayed before we ate. No matter what. It could be a full
fellowship dinner or cake and ice cream after a children's program.
Didn't matter what it was. Someone prayed. And sometimes the
prayers got lengthy, thanking God and asking Him to "bless this
food to the nourishment of our bodies."

One day, my mother, who was into healthy food choices,
made one of those stray comments adults make, forgetting who

might be listening. "Why are we thanking God for empty-calorie food like cookies and Kool-Aid?"

Well, because it tastes good. It gives us pleasure. God loves to give us good gifts. But the good-tasting and the good-for-us gifts both come from God. Wouldn't it be appropriate to give as much thanks for brussels sprouts as for brownies?

I admit. I've had some of those silly moments as I've bit into a square of scrumptious. "Oh, brownies. I love brownies. This is the best brownie I've ever eaten. Thank you, thank you, God, for creating chocolate because chocolate makes brownies and brownies are just so wonderful." My friends would laugh at my unfiltered delight and agree that chocolate was one of God's better ideas.

I don't think I could get away with the same song and dance about brussels sprouts. "Wow! Brussels sprouts! All that vitamin A and C and antioxidants that will make me stronger than Iron Man and smarter than Einstein. Thank you, God, for thinking up brussels sprouts." My friends would back away like I had contracted some contagious disease. I would wonder about my own emotional stability. No, no one goes off on a pleasure kick about brussels sprouts, even if we do like them.

I squirm when I read James's words: "Consider it pure joy, my brothers and sisters, whenever you face trials of many kinds" (James 1:2). Joy?

Trials aren't pleasant. They're *hard*! Why should I be joyful about the tough times—a basement flood, the work project with a one-week deadline rather than the expected one month, or unexpected company during that one week of extra work? The next verse gives the reason: "Because you know that the testing of your faith produces perseverance" (v. 3). The hardest moments of life produce the strongest kind of people.

We can give tacit agreement that hard work, hard anything, has its dividends, but must we joyfully thank God for it? God says yes, for James gives an example of how what we see as unpleasant can work to God's greater good a few verses later: "Believers in humble circumstances ought to take pride in their high position. But the rich should take pride in their humiliation—since they will pass away like a wildflower" (vv. 9–10). Our tendency is to believe that wealth is a good thing. It makes life easier, more pleasant. But James reverses the equation.

Those in poverty have the advantage of learning to trust God rather than themselves or others to provide their needs. And the rich? Wealth bears the lesson that riches don't satisfy every human longing like the poor might suspect. Only God can give us all we need or want.

A woman in labor well knows this contradiction between momentary pain and long-term payoff. She's able to endure arduous labor because joy will arrive soon in the form of a baby. She might be grinding her teeth in agony, but happy smiles come fast when that newborn is placed in her waiting arms.

We can thank God for what we have even when it's not on our top-ten list of favorite things. We can thank Him because we anticipate the good that will come from Him through what we have.

That basement flood can help me evaluate the possessions I've gripped too tightly. Unexpected company might bring deep conversations about God's place in our lives. And that pressure-cooker project invites us to depend on God's strength and provision to do what we initially view as impossible.

So when you and I hit a brussels-sprout moment or any level of distressing trial, we can lift our heads and say, "Lord, this has the potential to help me grow in ways that honor you and do great good for your kingdom. I thank you right now for how this unpleasant bit of life will bring about good both in my life and the lives of people around me. In fact, I'm looking forward to seeing what you're going to do with this mess."

We might even smile.

GRATITUDE PROMPT

What brussels-sprout moment are you facing? Thank God for what you are going through as an act of faith. Thank Him for His power and willingness to bring about greater good through any situation.

21

The Street Where I Live

The LORD himself goes before you and will be
with you; he will never leave you nor forsake you.
Do not be afraid; do not be discouraged.

DEUTERONOMY 31:8

I hate moving.
Wait. Change that. My mama would say, "Never say 'hate.'
Hate is too strong a word." So, in deference to Mama, I'll say, I
dislike moving. A lot.

Besides the physical strain of packing, loading, and unpacking,
and the stress of financing a new home, there's a genuine grief
process. Downsizing requires releasing long loved but no longer
needed stuff. We say goodbye to close friends, church family,
favorite restaurant hangouts, and overall community life to step
foot into a world of the unfamiliar that feels like culture shock.

It can be exciting at first, but then reality sets in and frustrations begin. Like finding a new hair stylist. A church family. New
doctors—did you transfer your medical records? By the end of
the day, you're tired and opt to eat out—but where? Nothing
looks familiar and your brain is too tired to work through cost
and calories. During one move, I tried not to complain, but my
longing came out in comments like, "Whoa, I could get breakfast

at our old diner for five bucks and this restaurant wants to charge me twelve dollars?"

Moving means a serpentine line of change points, and at the core, a lot of us don't like change—at least the parts we can't control. Life improvements are great if we have an idea beforehand of what they entail and can tailor them to our preferences. But the chaotic upheaval embedded within a move throws us into a new world of the unexpected and unfamiliar. Relocation requires us to put more effort into those daily moments we used to cruise through on autopilot.

My husband's and my last move was particularly hard for me. We moved fifteen hundred miles to a different climate and culture. I left some of the dearest friends I've had in my adult life. For several months, I inwardly grieved and chafed at the disruptions. Although we were returning to my hometown and moving closer to family, forty years had changed everything. I missed my previous house, my church, and the freedom to catch a cup of coffee at the five-dollar breakfast restaurant where the server knows me well enough to bring me coffee and my preferred small pitcher of two-percent milk without my needing to ask. I missed the familiar.

But God calls us to be thankful in all circumstances, even if a stranger now serves us a different blend of coffee and abruptly tells me to use the powdered creamer already on the table.

After days of staring at half-empty boxes, I determined to part the curtain of my gloom. So I put on my walking shoes and headed out, hoping to find something to thank God for on the street where I lived. I didn't even close the door of my new home before God hit the Golden Buzzer button and scattered sprinkles of His glory on everything around me.

That new home had been an incredible financial deal. We'd bought it sight unseen for half the asking price and had money left over for needed repairs and replacements. I looked across the tiny yard—a yard that my health-challenged husband didn't have to upkeep—and toward the house of our new neighbors who had helped us with an electrical issue the first weekend. I glanced across the street to the home of the cheerful neighbor whose little dog wore out his backend with wiggles whenever he saw me. My turn into the street startled a flock of doves feeding at our bird feeder. The brilliant blooms of a Mexican bird-of-paradise bush shouted for my attention, and the glorious view of the nine-thousand-foot mountain range begged me to belt out some song, any song, that proclaimed the greatness of our God.

My husband and I knew before we left our old house that God was prompting us to move. We saw the Lord at work before we put a padlock on the moving truck, preparing the way. And as the streets unfolded before us, we stepped into the halls of His golden goodness and feasted at the banqueting table of the becoming familiar.

Moving comes in many forms besides relocation. Your most recent move might be from work to retirement, health to illness, full house to empty nest and sometimes empty arms. The grief over the loss is palpable. The daily little changes taunt you with what you used to have. But here you are on a new street.

My friend, God walks that street with you. He's gone before you to get everything ready. He invites you to take His hand and explore the new street with Him. As you do, He'll show you the greatness of His glory—if you're willing to put on your walking shoes and search for it.

How grateful I am that God has promised in His Word to go before us and walk with us. We don't need to be discouraged or overly stressed, because He knows all about our new place in life, and He is as near as our next breath of prayer. But gratitude for change takes intentionality. If you've moved into a new season of life, step out your door. Explore the street where you live. Look for what God has waiting for you and how He has prepared the way for you. Then take His hand, thank Him for His presence with you, and explore your new world.

It will be better than any shower of Golden Buzzer confetti.

GRATITUDE PROMPT

Take a walk or peek out your window. Look around you. What blessings has God given you? Make a list and thank God for each one.

PART THREE

See What God Has Done

Come and hear, all you who fear God; let
me tell you what he has done for me.

Psalm 66:16

When God does the remarkable within our ordinary, He
gives us a story to tell and a chance to tell the story.

22

God's Construction Zone

Sing the praises of the LORD, enthroned in Zion;
proclaim among the nations what he has done.

PSALM 9:11

"Small Town," Illinois, where my husband served as senior minister at a local church for ten years, is a town of one thousand residents, out in the middle of a patchwork of corn and soybean fields. Yet the church leadership had the ostentatious dream to build a gym to the west of the sanctuary and educational building.

At least some church members thought it was an outrageous idea. The congregation didn't need such a facility. This is a small town. It would never be used. And they didn't have the projected $800,000 to build such a project. Opposition grew. Someone even threatened to never set foot in that structure—if it ever happened, which they doubted.

The congregation built it anyway. The $800,000 was paid off in less than two years. And in the time my husband and I served at that little church, we saw the gym and its adjoining spacious kitchen used for youth activities, Wednesday night meals that drew regular crowds of over one hundred hungry townspeople, and special events. The facility became a huge draw for wedding receptions, funeral dinners, and farm co-op annual meetings.

91

One fundraiser to help pay the medical bills of our local funeral director's daughter, who had been born with a heart defect, drew nearly four hundred people. A Halloween alternative brought 275 children and parents. We heard stories the next year of parents who took their children trick-or-treating, and the children begged, "Can we just go to the church?"

The church grew, and people came to faith in Christ because the congregation had added more doors of entry and used what God gave them to reach out to the needs of a small farming community.

The story of "Small Town" parallels the biblical account of Nehemiah, a cupbearer to the Persian king. Nehemiah heard about the broken walls surrounding the city of Jerusalem. He saw a need, knew something could be done, and made himself available to do it. After much prayer and sharing his dream with the king, Nehemiah headed toward his home country to spearhead the rebuilding efforts.

Construction was not easy. Locals didn't want the project to succeed. They laughed. They taunted. "What they are building—even a fox climbing up on it would break down their wall of stones!" (Nehemiah 4:3). Yet the Israelite work force prevailed. At every step they witnessed the hand of God partnering with them to complete their task. They finished the wall in a record fifty-two days, and the impact on their enemies was incredible. "All the surrounding nations were afraid and lost their self-confidence, because they realized that this work had been done with the help of our God" (6:16). And the quality of their work? Those walls that couldn't hold a fox withstood the weight of hundreds of worshipers marching on top as they gave praise to God, praise loud enough for neighboring cities to hear the uproar (12:43).

I've witnessed accounts similar to Nehemiah's story throughout my life. God working through and among a group of people to bring about incredible results for good, despite tremendous odds and greater opposition. Churches rising from the ashes of literal fires to grow and strengthen in ways they had never known before. Parachurch organizations starting because God put a dream in the heart of a most unlikely person with miniscule resources, and those small beginnings burst into large national, even international, ministries.

And my own story. Legally blind since birth, receiving never-before sight at age fifty-five and then having the privilege of telling hundreds of people what God has done for me.

"Come and see what the Lord has done" (Psalm 46:8).

"For what you have done I will always praise you" (52:9).

"Let me tell you what he has done for me" (66:16).

You can't think of what God has done for you? Oh yes, maybe you have the little daily, generalized blessings everyone gets, but nothing as spectacular as an international ministry or incredible healing. Yet God works within each of us to bring about His good purposes (Philippians 2:13). All of us are involved in some way in God's story. The people of "Small Town," Nehemiah, and I will all tell you we were not solo acts. Many people stood beside us and took part in what God did to bring about incredible results.

God delights to give each of us a story worth telling and then a chance to tell the story. Some stories may look as expansive as the Grand Canyon; others might seem as common but as intricate as the layered petals of a rose. Whatever your story, it deserves more than a notecard of thanks to our great God. It merits dancing on the walls, or dancing under the stars as I did the first time I saw the night sky with my new eyesight. It might be as simple as clasping your hands with delight as you witness someone you've mentored move on to bigger beginnings than you ever dreamed possible.

Whatever joyful expression you can give for how God has used you to be an influence in His kingdom work, do it. Give thanks. Tell what God has done!

GRATITUDE PROMPT

What story has God given you? What God-sized adventure have you taken part in with others? Ask God to refresh your memory of those times you witnessed Him do great things when you made yourself available to Him. Then thank Him—joyfully!

23

Pick-Up Service

For what you have done I will always praise you
in the presence of your faithful people. And I will
hope in your name, for your name is good.

PSALM 52:9

I love stories. I especially love stories that tell of God's work in
the world, and His interaction and participation in the finer
details of our lives. How, if we look beyond the actual event, we
can see God as part of the story. How He shows up in wonderful,
miraculous ways that we can attribute only to Him.

I love God's sense of timing. I love His above-and-beyond
provision. And I love His better-than-ever power that speaks of
His existence, continuing presence, and unfailing love.

Like the pick-up services at grocery stores.

Yes, I use pick-up and delivery services. I feel rich. Pampered.
Almost guilty that I have someone else do the hard work of pulling stuff off the shelf, loading it in baskets, and hauling it to my
car or front door. Yet when I think of the events that merged so
I could have this service, the credit belongs to God.

Before the COVID pandemic, grocery pickup and delivery
service was in its infancy. Then the call for social distancing
catapulted it into popularity. During the height of the pandemic,

my husband and I lived in a rural area too far from stores that offered the service to make it work for us. Then we moved to the big city, where our two favorite stores were less than two miles from our house. Shortly after we moved, my husband's health issues increased. Jack found it painful to follow me around in a store, and some days he couldn't even drive. But I couldn't drive because of my limited eyesight. We could manage any one of these issues individually, but thrown together, shopping in-store became nearly impossible.

It was around that time that pickup and delivery service became more user friendly. Our two favorite stores offered perks and discounts that made it affordable for us. We ventured forth to try the service and quickly wondered how we had managed without it. What had looked for years like a luxury now bordered on necessity.

I'll take it further than that. It was a gift from God. I don't deserve pickup and delivery service. I could manage on my own, even though it would be hard. But God, in His grace and mercy, shows His care for me by providing that for me.

Does God really work like that? Doesn't He have loftier things to deal with than a couple's need for groceries?

Some people may look at menial tasks like grocery shopping as part of ordinary life, too insignificant for God's concern. But I truly do believe that when we commit our lives to God, He becomes part of our life story. His Holy Spirit is now within us, and He partners with us to influence our corner of the world and to bring us all the way to our eternal home. He will provide all we need to make that happen in His time, in His way. Even if it involves shopping.

God's provision for His children shows the rest of the world that He's taking care of us. Our stories give evidence of His existence and character, that He really is a good, kind, compassionate God who takes personal interest in everything happening to us. God's methods of taking care of us are as numerous and varied as the thousands of flower varieties that color our earth. Jesus said in His Sermon on the Mount that God would take care of us with the same lavish attention that He spills over a meadow of many-splendored wildflowers (Matthew 6:28–30).

Is it possible, even conceivable, that God could converge the popularity of pick-up service with our specific need? Absolutely! For us and many others. He can do that because He is God.

An initial step in embracing a life of gratitude is to recognize God's participation in your life. If you have trouble distinguishing God's involvement in the small moments, ask Him to show you. Pray, "Lord, give me a story to tell." Ask Him to demonstrate in no uncertain terms how He provides for you every day.

Then thank Him for the little things: parking spots near a store's entrance, a series of green lights as you travel to an appointment, a friend's encouraging Facebook meme posted on a particularly hard day, or a surprise sale on your favorite apple variety. They are all gifts from your heavenly Father, who loves to take care of you in splendid ways, especially on the hard days when you need an extra hug from Him.

When we pause to thank Him for the gifts of life that aren't that necessary but are oh, so nice, our days grow brighter with the light of His goodness.

GRATITUDE PROMPT

What benefit has come your way at just the right time? Consider it a gift from God. Whisper a thank you, and then pray for the chance to tell someone the story.

24

Computers

Many, Lord my God,
are the wonders you have done,
the things you planned for us.
None can compare with you;
were I to speak and tell of your deeds,
they would be too many to declare.

PSALM 40:5

Computers are wonderful—when they work. And when they
don't? I growl that gremlins are dancing on my motherboard,
laughing at my frustration.

On those rare occasions when my printer connection fails or
worse yet, I lose a file, I remind myself how God has used computers in my life as a testimony of His faithfulness.

Hear me out. I'm serious.

I made it through undergraduate school using an antique
Smith Corona manual typewriter when fellow classmates had
electric typewriters. At the time, the visual acuity in my better
eye measured a mere 20/200 on good days. In real life terms, I
sat hunched over the typewriter, my face three inches from the
piece of paper to see what I was typing. Because I have no depth
perception, I never could dab Wite-Out on the exact spot of a

typo. I could have bought an electric typewriter with the paper I wasted typing pages over again.

Then I entered grad school, and my program required a thesis. Typing out a two-hundred-page paper on even my husband's electric typewriter would have been visually impossible. Yes, I could have hired a typist, but I would have found it challenging to put my manuscript in a type-ready format. However, only two years before, Apple had released the Apple 2E, and it was now at a price we sacrificially could afford. The timing was perfect. I don't think I could have completed my thesis without that computer.

Ten years later found my writing career exploding in a new direction. But the 2E was old. Personal computers had become more affordable and useable, but I couldn't see the screen of my husband's new Microsoft 486SX. Within a year, though, someone connected me with our state's rehabilitation services, which provided me with my own computer, a huge hunker of a twenty-four-inch monitor, and screen magnification software. The equipment didn't merely make writing easier; it made it possible.

Over the next twenty years, technology advanced at a steady rate, finally outdistancing my magnification software. Laptops and tablets equipped with built-in magnification allowed me to take my work with me even as my writing career took another giant leap forward. Today, the accessibility features on laptops and smart phone have busted open the doors for not only me but countless others who deal with disabilities. Computer innovations have made it possible to be productive and keep pace with the rest of the world.

If the intersecting of technology advances and my visual needs had happened once, we could chalk it up to coincidence. Twice? "Ain't technology grand?" people would say to me.

But four distinct times? I choose to believe it was the hand of God. He knows my needs. He's called me to write. He has and will provide what I need to do what He's asked me to do.

When we pray, we often look for one-time, straight-line answers to our prayers. We often do see God showing up in marvelous ways, giving us a simple plot to tell: See what God has done. But at other times, God's story is in epic form, told over the span of years in a way that reveals His consistent faithfulness. He's always there for us, constantly providing, and continually aware of what we need to live life according to His promises.

You may have normal vision. You may never put your fingers on a laptop keyboard. But look for God in the pages of your own story. What consistent theme do you see? It might be in the chapters of illness, financial stress, or child raising. Has God provided cars, homes, or other high-dollar items at the right time in the right price range? How has He done it not just once but enough times to call it a pattern?

The beauty of God's faithfulness is this: If He's provided for you in amazing ways multiple times before, He will do it again. The apostle Paul expressed that hope when he wrote his second letter to the Corinthian church: "He has delivered us from such a deadly peril, and he will deliver us again. On him we have set our hope that he will continue to deliver us" (2 Corinthians 1:10). If you read the list of Paul's adventures in 2 Corinthians 11:24–27, you'll see that he experienced enough deadly perils for several lifetimes, and yet he still retained every confidence in God. He knew firsthand that God delivers.

And if you're tempted to worry or grumble when things glitch on you—like printer hiccups and lost files—you can recall how God has provided in the past. Then combine gratitude with trust, thanking Him that if He's done something gracious for you before, He can and will do a repeat performance.

He's that good.

GRATITUDE PROMPT

How has God reliably provided for you at the right time? Thank Him for His consistent faithfulness.

25

Restaurant Worker

I will tell of the kindnesses of the LORD,
the deeds for which he is to be praised,
according to all the LORD has done for us—
yes, the many good things
he has done for Israel,
according to his compassion and many kindnesses.

ISAIAH 63:7

Some days you feel awful enough to not have any shame about your personal appearance. That's how I felt the day my husband and I walked into a Denny's restaurant in Zanesville, Ohio. We were returning home the day after I'd had eye muscle surgery in Columbus. Bandages covered both eyes and I was in pain. I just wanted to go home.

My husband and I both knew, however, that life would go into high gear once we traveled the sixty more miles to our home. Jack does not manage kitchen responsibilities well, so he suggested we grab lunch before we reached home. Inwardly I fretted. I couldn't see a thing. Jack would have to do everything for me in view of an entire dining room at high noon. And what restaurant server would be patient enough with a woman who would probably spill lunch over her already disheveled front?

My worry was pointless. My kind heavenly Father had already prepared the way.

Our server—I think her name was Ashley—greeted us with compassion, led us to the nearest available table, gave us time for Jack to read the menu to me, and then went above and beyond her job description. She positioned my sandwich plate in front of me, describing the orientation of the food on my plate. She checked back often, each time giving me verbal cues, speaking in a quiet voice only I could hear.

I've dealt with vision issues long enough to guess she had experience with someone who couldn't see. But what I remember most is her gentle voice. She spoke kindly and quietly, in a way that would not draw attention to my situation.

When I walked into that restaurant, I felt discouraged and anxious. Would the surgery help? Would my family and church let me off the hook while I recovered? How would I manage over the next few weeks? I needed a dose of reassurance, and God dished up a triple scoop through Ashley's kind actions and words.

I wonder if Ruth from the Bible felt that way. In the book named after her, you'll find the story of how she'd lost her husband and father-in-law. She'd traveled to a foreign country with her despondent mother-in-law, Naomi. They were impoverished, so Ruth did the one thing poor women could do in that society—she gathered leftover grain in the sight of everybody and their brother.

Among those who noticed her, one person saw not a poor woman but a brave woman trying to do her best—and that someone reached out to her in kindness. The wealthy landowner Boaz protected Ruth from further scrutiny by encouraging her to glean only in his fields. He treated her with respect, like she was one of his female workers, not a destitute foreigner. He provided water and not just a little food but triple scoops of grain.

The discouraged mother-in-law Naomi noticed his kindness and was grateful for it. "The LORD bless him," she said. "He has not stopped showing his kindness to the living and the dead" (Ruth 2:20). Naomi made the connection that God was showing kindness to them through the words and actions of Boaz.

Life's hardships are easier to bear when someone shoulders the load with us. A word, a touch, five seconds of centering a plate—all take miniscule bits of time and effort. When we're on the giving end of kindness, we dismiss what we do: "It was nothing. I wish I could do much more." But when we're on the receiving end, that little bit tells us someone notices and cares. We know what the giver doesn't—that those little grace notes came when we needed them the most. My server, Ashley, could see the bandages on my eyes, but she didn't know my emotional state. God took her skills with customers and placed her exactly where I needed her.

No life event has a straight-line plot. Stories are a series of scenes that lead to the final, big conclusion. It's true in fiction; it's true in real life. God does more than simply solve our problems or deliver us from danger. The little kind actions we take fit into the larger context of a life story. Only God, the master choreographer, could have arranged the scenes in such a perfect order.

It's a good thing I'm not God. If I were in charge, my solution would be to prevent problems from happening in the first place. Instead, as God works behind the scenes to lead us through the obstacles of life, He adds in bonus gifts of smaller stories. And He sends helpers in human form who bear gifts earmarked with His kindness and grace. All the more story material for us to shout, "See what God has done!"

When life becomes overwhelming, think of the people God has sent you to share the hardship. It might be providing a meal you don't have to fix, doing a job too difficult for you at the time, or sending a text that assures you of their prayers. You may not need their physical help, but their action and words communicate they care, and God has sent them to be ambassadors of His kindness and grace.

GRATITUDE PROMPT

Who has shown you kindness in the last week, no matter how small? Make a list and thank God twice—for the person and for God's kindness in sending that person to you.

26

Answered Prayer

Let us then approach God's throne of grace with
confidence, so that we may receive mercy and
find grace to help us in our time of need.

HEBREWS 4:16

My daughter texted a nonchalant reason for her tardiness
to her toddler's play group. The accompanying photo was
worse than the explanation, and my husband and I responded
with the typical parental knee jerk. "Oh, my!" A truck had caught
fire on the interstate, causing a four-mile traffic backup. Her
continuing reports made the news more alarming. As she inched
her car through the traffic jam, she passed a fresh accident where
one car had not braked soon enough and plowed into another car.

It gave me shivers. A mile closer, a few minutes before, and
she and our grandson could have been . . . I didn't want to think
it. "I'm thankful for God's protection of you," I texted back then
headed toward the kitchen. Midstep, I wheeled a U-turn and
faced my husband.

"Didn't you pray for our family's safety this morning?"

Jack often prays for our family during our mealtime prayer,
but this morning, he had prayed specifically for safety. Not that I
was paying attention. I admit, I'm often thinking of what I forgot
to put on the table rather than tuning in enough to remember
prayer content hours later.

But God heard. And remembered. And responded. Big time. Genesis 24 contains one of my favorite Bible stories. A mere twenty-four chapters into the Bible, the biblical account tells of God's response to a request about a life matter that, at first glance, could hardly be called a weighty spiritual matter—romance! Abraham sent his servant to find a wife for his son Isaac among his extended family clan. But the servant was a tad nervous about such a huge responsibility, so he prayed. It was an audacious prayer: specific, detailed. He prayed that the young woman he asked for a drink at the community well would not only give him a drink but also offer to give water to his camels and that the woman who did so would be the right choice for Isaac's new bride.

That is exactly what happened. He hadn't even finished praying when Rebekah approached the well. He asked. She gave. She offered to water his camels and didn't stop till the camels had their fill. Considering the capacity of camels for water containment, that must have taken a good amount of time and hard work. The servant asked if he might stay at her home, a reasonable request in that culture. Rebekah went beyond the request to assure him they had plenty for both him and his camels.

God not only answered the servant's prayer, but He put two exclamation marks on His answer when the servant had asked for only a period. I know God answers prayer like that. I've seen Him do it. He gives better-than-ever, more than we can possibly imagine, above and beyond what we expect.

Praise would impulsively pour from my mouth if I saw the direct connection between my prayers and God's answers. But I can't see God's answers if I pray generalized or rote prayers that I can't remember. Spontaneous thanks is more apt to happen when we pray intentional and specific prayers.

Perhaps we're afraid to be as bold as Abraham's servant. Maybe we've prayed specifically, and we don't know why God has answered no. We don't like refusals, so we don't ask again. But the reason might be that we aren't on God's timetable, or we've asked with wrong motives. More often, we may simply be looking in the wrong direction and can't see how God is working and moving far beyond our initial request.

If we want to see God's mighty power at work, our prayers need to be intentional, specific, and deliberate. Pay attention to how you pray. What exactly would you like God to do? Are you asking in a way that you will see His answer when it happens?

Then, after you've prayed, be equally intentional in looking for God's answers. I've found myself praying for God's guidance in a situation at the beginning of my day. Then I get busy, the problem resolves itself, and I forget that I asked for God's help. If I record my prayers on paper and then review them at day's end, asking myself, "How did God help me in this?" I'm more apt to see His answers and be motivated to give Him thanks.

Specific prayer is risky. You run the risk of not getting what you thought you needed. But then again, you might. And in the process of prayer, you'll learn about the character and motives of this God who can do anything. You'll discover how to structure your prayers to fit His agenda. You'll pay more attention to what you're asking for. And as you grow in your awareness of how to interact with God, you'll do U-turns in the middle of your moments as you turn to thank Him for doing such marvelous things.

Come boldly before His throne. Ask. Seek. Remember the moment. The Lord will show you He's listening. He'll give you a "See what the Lord has done" kind of story. And the praise will spill from your overflowing heart.

GRATITUDE PROMPT

Buy a composition notebook. Record your prayer requests on the left side. Save room on the right side for recording God's answers. Dare to be specific in what you request.

27

Waiting Prayer

Do not be anxious about anything, but in
every situation, by prayer and petition, with
thanksgiving, present your requests to God.

PHILIPPIANS 4:6

Stephen, a global evangelism worker, knew firsthand what
it was like to wait for God to answer prayer. His wife and
ministry partner, Shanthi, had cancer, and doctors had tried all
the treatment methods they knew. Stephen and countless others
had prayed for Shanthi for months. All of us waited for some
sign of improvement.

On one of his furlough visits, Stephen shared with my local
church what happened next. He'd been praying fervently for
Shanthi's healing for many months. Then he read Philippians
4:6, where Paul encourages his readers to pray about everything
with thanksgiving. What if, Stephen asked himself, instead of
asking God to heal Shanthi, he thanked God for what God was
going to do?

His story intrigued me. For years I'd followed the little formula
ACTS in my prayer life—Adoration, Confession, Thanksgiving, and Supplication. I had one list for requests and one list
for thanksgiving. Both lists held different items. This was new.

Thanking God in advance for what He was going to do? Weaving thanks into what I was asking God for at the time I prayed, not after, when God answered?

Other Scripture shows Stephen was on the right track. Paul's letters to the various churches all start with a prayer, often laced with thanks for that group of people. All four gospels record that Jesus gave thanks *before* the disciples distributed the five loaves and two fish of a boy's lunch to feed five thousand people. Jesus thanked God *before* He raised Lazarus from the dead (John 11:41–42), not afterward.

Waiting for God to move on our requests feels harder than a child waiting for Christmas. We begin to overthink, wondering if God is capable. Maybe He's not interested in what we're facing. Some of us navel gaze, fretting that the problem is us: we don't deserve God's abundance. Or maybe we didn't use the proper words that would magically release the lock on God's goodness.

Weaving thanks into our prayer requests isn't a magic formula to cause God to answer more quickly. But saying thank you for the thing you desire communicates some powerful messages. Gratitude in advance shows we're confident that God listens, cares, and acts on our behalf. When Jesus prayed at Lazarus's tomb, he said, "Father, I thank you that you have heard me" (John 11:41). When we follow Jesus's example and thank God for hearing us, we push back the temptation to believe He isn't listening or doesn't care.

While we wait for God's answer to our requests, we can thank God for what He is going to do. I call it prophetic thanks. Thanking God in advance demonstrates our faith and trust in a God who is and will be good to us, no matter how He chooses to respond. The Bible doesn't record that Jesus thanked God for His plan to fill twelve baskets with leftovers. It simply says that Jesus gave thanks. We too can say, "Thank you, God, for *whatever* you plan to do. I trust you to do what is best, and I'm anticipating that it will be something fantastic."

In the meantime, we can thank God for His concern, power, and unfailing love. No matter how our life situation resolves, God is still God. He is powerful and good. He loves us and wants the best for us. Thanking Him during the wait shows that, come what may, we're grateful God is part of our life and that He is in control.

Are you in a waiting season? Do you wonder if God is working behind the scenes or if He hears you? Perhaps you've wondered if you've missed the mark and are praying for the wrong thing. Minutes pass, then months, as you wait for something, anything, to happen that will give you hope for a better life.

May I encourage you to stop and say thank you to your Lord? Thank Him for who He is and for His power and desire to do what you have asked for in His name. Thank Him for His wisdom in knowing what is best for you. Tell Him you are excited to see what He will do. Show awe that He has the creativity to come up with such original answers that all those around you will know God was the only one who could pull it off. Then tell Him thanks for walking with you through whatever you face, and for His promise that He will never, ever abandon you.

Pairing requests with gratitude isn't guaranteed to shorten God's response time. You may still need to wait. But the wait will no longer fill you with doubt and anxiety. Through your expressed gratitude, you've reminded yourself and the Lord that you are confident He will give you His best.

GRATITUDE PROMPT

What are you waiting for? Thank God for what He plans to do. Thank Him for His love for you that never gives up until He accomplishes His will for you.

28

Wise Words

The Sovereign LORD has given me a well-instructed tongue,
to know the word that sustains the weary.

ISAIAH 50:4

I forget that my mother has developing dementia. When she speaks with critical words, I wonder why she must be cranky about petty things. I answer her blunt requests and questions with impatience. Then I remember that aging has changed the woman I know and love, and I become more frustrated—not at her, because she can't control the unfiltered comments, but at myself for not coming up with better responses.

All of us have been there. We feel inept in knowing how to respond to the unexpected comments and criticisms from stranger, friend, or family. If only we could have a five-minute warning so we had time to prepare a witty, wise, and winsome comeback.

Our enemy, Satan, is subtle in his attempts to bring us down and cause us to say the wrong thing at the wrong time. When someone challenges our understanding of the Bible, we stall, wishing our pastor was at our elbow to take on those questions we can't answer. And the everyday moments within our family can further corrode our confidence. If Mother's loud comment about my choice of dress for church leaves me with a gaping, silent mouth, what makes me think I can come up with any sensible thing to someone who asks me about the hope I have in Christ?

Jesus once reassured His disciples, "I will give you words and wisdom that none of your adversaries will be able to resist or contradict" (Luke 21:15). "It will not be you speaking," Jesus promised, "but the Spirit of your Father speaking through you" (Matthew 10:20).

Would God's help also be available to me whenever I want to represent Him well in my speech but find myself at a loss for words? David prayed that the words of his mouth and the meditations of his heart would be acceptable to God (Psalm 19:14). Don't I want that as well? Don't I want to know how to graciously, lovingly respond to the careless, casual comments I face in my everyday moments?

After one impatient episode with my mother that left me in shame for my harsh comeback, I prayed specifically that God would fill my mouth with kind words. God did it! The next time I visited, Mother made a barbed comment. And the impulsive words I spoke in response were not my own. I'm not that smart or godly. The words were gracious and winsome, and they made her laugh.

It wasn't an isolated incident. God has given me words when counseling hurting women, the right choice of words when encountering someone who wants to sell me a false gospel, and a gentle response to a family member who woke up on the wrong side of the bed. I know myself. On the inside I feel frustrated and irritable, but when I've asked God, the words that come out of my mouth are God-honoring.

Remember Nehemiah, the governor who helped the Jewish exiles rebuild the walls of Jerusalem? He experienced God's wise intervention too. The Bible tells us that when the king inquired about the troubled look on Nehemiah's face. Nehemiah had the courage to fill the space with a silent pause. He prayed. Then he spoke. The words must have been appropriate, for amazingly, the king gave him what he asked for and more besides. God guided Nehemiah to say the right words at the right time (Nehemiah 2:1–6).

Isn't that awesome? God, the source of all wisdom who will always say the perfect thing, is willing to put His Spirit within us so He can speak through us. But I'm prone to overthink. If my mother laughed one time, and other times she doesn't, did I fail? Did God fail? Maybe I wasn't listening well to His voice, and I said something not quite right.

If we have prayed for the right words, we can thank God for putting His words in our mouths no matter how others respond. Their reaction is not an indication that we have failed. In fact, the truth, even spoken in love, might increase people's anger because they don't want to hear it. Jesus predicted this. Condemnations may continue even after we have spoken (Luke 21:12–19). Have you noticed that your listeners might initially respond with arguments and anger, but with time, the Holy Spirit sinks your words into their spirits, and upon reflection, those people change their position?

I find it amazing and humbling that the God of the universe wants to interact with me and put His words in my mouth. You and I can thank Him for making His wisdom available to us so we can speak words of peace that represent Him well.

GRATITUDE PROMPT

Do you face a potential situation where you don't know what to say or how to respond? Pray, asking God for the words to say and thanking Him that He wants to partner with you to speak the best words for that situation.

29

Paths of Protection

Let all who take refuge in you be glad;
let them ever sing for joy.
Spread your protection over them,
that those who love your name may rejoice in you.
PSALM 5:11

When I was a teenager, I rode a bike. In my neighborhood.
Down bike paths. On busy streets. No helmet.

Remember, I'm the one who was legally blind until I was fifty-five.

Early on, when I was ten, I crashed my bike in an alley strewn with gravel. A skinned knee was my reward. But the incident only made me more determined to keep trying. In the ensuing years, I never had another bicycle accident.

I was stubborn. I wanted to be like everyone else. And I made unwise decisions regarding my choice of routes. I deserved to be in a bad, even fatal accident. Considering road conditions, I likely had several near misses.

I can only attest my safety record to the mercy of God.

His mercy was more apparent the day when I, as an adult, went on a bike outing with a group from my church on a rough trail in northern Ohio. When oncoming bikers passed us, my lack of depth perception caused me to misjudge the drop-off on my right, and I felt my bike wobble and tip. I bore down and kept going, miraculously staying upright when I and my bike should have ended up in a tangled mess at the bottom of the ravine.

That had to have been God's protection.

Several passages in Psalms compare God's protection to that of a refuge. I envision David's inspiration came from the times he hid in a cave during those years he was on the run from murderous King Saul. David once wrote, "From the ends of the earth I call to you, I call as my heart grows faint; lead me to the rock that is higher than I" (Psalm 61:2). If you're hiding in a cave with a storm brewing outside or a pitched battle on the flatlands below, you will hear only the muffled sounds of the storm or battle. If you step to the entrance, you'll see the carnage and chaos. But you won't be harmed. You are protected by the strength and security of the rock face.

God's protection is like that. His presence wraps around us like an invisible shield, blocking those things that could destroy us. We see the danger, but we don't necessarily see the One who stands between us and what could harm us. It is only when the crisis has passed and we realize what could have happened that we realize the extent of God's protection.

God gave the prophet Elisha's servant a glimpse of God's protective force in the account found in 2 Kings 6:8–17. An enemy army had surrounded the city where Elisha lived. Out for morning errands, the servant ran home to Elisha. "What shall we do?"

Elisha prayed that God would open the servant's eyes to see beyond the seen. Then the servant saw God at work. The hills beyond the city held flaming chariots and horsemen that could only be a host of heavenly beings. They had been there all along, even when the servant could see only the enemy. God was protecting the city whether the servant could see the angel army or not. In the same way, God safeguards us in ways we will not see most of the time.

When others tell us how God has protected them, it's tempting to dismiss what they say. How do we know it was God's hand at work and not just sheer luck? Maybe the situation was not as severe as they make it sound. Perhaps I was a better bike rider than I thought, and my skill kept me from careening down that hill.

If I have avoided harm, I'd rather err on the side of giving God credit for His protection than not. And I wonder if at times He allows us to get closer than comfortable to harmful situations so we can see how serious He is about taking care of us. Those near misses—arriving five minutes behind a fatal car crash, stuck one mile behind a burning truck, or staying atop an out-of-control bicycle—give evidence to us and our listeners of the protective power of God.

Some will point out the times God seemed to fail at protecting them from harm. Why did God safeguard me from a bike accident and not someone else?

All of us will at some point in our lives experience hardship, suffering, even death. We live in a fallen world, and all humans will suffer the unintended consequences of their own or others' poor choices. In the final section of this book, we'll look at how to stay grateful in the worst of times. For now, however, let's not let the worst-case scenarios distract us from God's promises to be our refuge or the evidence of those moments when His protection is obvious.

How He chooses to shelter us is up to Him. Those moments of danger give us opportunities to depend on Him, seek His wisdom, and allow Him to use a difficult situation for His ultimate glory. And for those who claim faith in Christ, death will never be the final blow. We live in the sphere of eternity, and God will never allow anything to crush our souls. Until that time when we transfer from earth to eternity, God holds the moments of our lives in His hands. He will not allow trouble or trial to have center stage until He is ready to work within the moment of suffering to bring us onward to himself. In those worst of times, if we look closely, we will see how, even within the suffering, God prevented the situation from fully crushing or engulfing us.

If you fear a potentially dangerous situation, you can thank God in advance that He has the power to protect you—whether from turbulence during a thunderstorm-strewn air flight, an explosion of violence on your neighborhood street, or a stretch of highway that has been the site of several fatal accidents in recent months. If danger seems imminent, God invites you to thank Him for His power to protect you. And if tragedy does impact you, hindsight will reveal how and how much God did protect you from greater harm.

As you face any danger, you can pray, "Lord, give me a story to tell that will lead others to thank you for doing what only you can do."

GRATITUDE PROMPT

Thank God for protecting you daily in ways you cannot see. Thank Him that He will continue to provide the security that is more solid than the rock face of a hillside cave.

30

Salvation

Truly my soul finds rest in God;
my salvation comes from him.

PSALM 62:1

As my children grew, my prayers for them became more impassioned. One evening, overwhelmed with the kind of world they were entering and mindful of the words from the Lord's Prayer, "deliver us from the evil one" (Matthew 6:13), I prayed in front of them, "Oh God, deliver my children from the evil forces of this world."

I kissed my girls good night and shut the door. Five minutes later, I heard wails from my older daughter. I burst through the door. "Katherine! What's wrong?"

She choked on her sobs. "Mommy, I'm scared of those evil horses you prayed about."

Horses are real, something a seven-year-old can understand. But how could I explain the elusive dangers embedded within the spiritual world or the grip of the devil's scheme to suck us under? For that matter, was I ready to explain how sin has messed up our world and how, despite my best parenting efforts, my sweet children would need saving from sin like anyone else?

The Bible speaks often about God's plan to bring us back to

himself after Adam and Eve disobeyed God's one command. Throughout Scripture, God uses imagery of rescue, deliverance, and salvation to help us internalize how Jesus's death on the cross creates a bridge that allows us to reconnect with Him.

Our minds glitch on the word *save*. Do I need saving? If life on earth is going well, what do I need to be saved from? How can I be thankful for something I don't think I need?

Unfortunately sin destroys us, shattering the image of God that He imprinted upon our nature. Even one sin leaves a stain on our soul we cannot remove, and no one is perfect, which means every human is forever placed away from God. Worse, no amount of attempted right living on our part would ever be enough to make us right with God (Titus 3:4–6).

But God longs to rescue us from the death and destruction sin causes. So God made a plan to save us. Jesus's purpose in coming into the world, the angel told Joseph, was to "save his people from their sins" (Matthew 1:21). Because of God's great love for us, He would do anything to draw us back to himself. That "anything" meant sending Jesus to die on the cross.

When Jesus relinquished his life for our sake, he set free those who put their faith in Him. Imagine Jesus standing at the gates of hell, relinquishing His life so we could run past a dying Jesus into heaven's eternity.

God's infinite power can save us from any peril. Even a seven-year-old can understand rescue from danger. Yet God goes far beyond the physical. Yes, He can and does sometimes rescue us from evil situations and wicked people. But His greatest gift is the plan He has already set in place to save us from sin. No matter how deep the hole is that you've dug for yourself, or how greatly the knots of your own life choices constrain you, God wants to pull you out of the mess and lead you into the halls of heaven.

Salvation is your best story.

You might find that hard to internalize. I know I do. There's a part of us that wants visual proof and present experience. After all,

Jesus's death happened two thousand years ago. So while the Bible tells us we are saved, still, if we haven't had a life-altering salvation experience like we hear about from others, it's easy to doubt the significance of this best gift. Shouldn't we have felt something?

I'm intrigued by how many times the psalmists recollect the marvelous miracles God did in rescuing His people from Egypt. They write as if it were part of their life experience. Yet at least eight hundred years span the time from Moses, the leader of the Israelites, to David, one of the chief writers of the Psalms. David's generation of writers believed the written and oral records that told how God had done mighty things to bring the nation of Israel out of Egypt into a land of their own (Psalm 105).

You didn't stand at the cross two thousand years ago. But Jesus still saved you. You may not have felt anything emotionally when you decided to turn about-face and center your life around Jesus. Yet a transformation process began that day as the Holy Spirit worked with your spirit to recreate your life back into the image of God. No matter how rotten life is right now or how much the world descends into chaos, God will save you at the end of time. No matter what you see to the contrary, if you believe Jesus is the savior of your soul, He has done this great thing for you. He has given you salvation.

How do we respond to such a great salvation? We live lives of gratitude for what the Lord has done. He has rescued us from the destructive force of sin. He will deliver us from eternal death.

God's gift of salvation is worth every ounce of thanks you can offer. For it really is your best story to tell.

GRATITUDE PROMPT

Start a gratitude list in your prayer journal. Write at the top, "My salvation." Thank God every day this week that He provided the way to save you from sin's destructive forces.

PART FOUR

Seeing beyond the Seen

Praise be to the God and Father of our Lord Jesus
Christ, who has blessed us in the heavenly realms
with every spiritual blessing in Christ.

EPHESIANS 1:3

No one and nothing can take away the spiritual blessings
God has waiting for you.

31

Forgiveness

> He has rescued us from the dominion of darkness and
> brought us into the kingdom of the Son he loves, in
> whom we have redemption, the forgiveness of sins.
>
> Colossians 1:13–14

Forgiveness is the premiere of the spiritual blessings God has waiting for us. Our salvation is not complete without forgiveness.

Imagine two neighbors at odds with each other. Bill holds a long-standing grudge against Jason. Both men are decent guys and used to be buddies. But one Saturday, Jason's dog trampled Bill's vegetable garden. And Bill has never let Jason forget it.

Another Saturday, Bill hears a loud crash. Peeking over the fence, he sees Jason sprawled on the ground in a pool of blood, a ladder collapsed on top of him. Bill jumps the fence, uses his shirt to stanch the blood, and calls 911. Bill's quick actions save Jason's life, the EMT crew tell Jason.

Does that change anything? No. Bill remains hostile. Jason has tried to thank Bill for saving his life and to rebuild a neighborly relationship, but Bill stays at arm's length.

Wait a minute, you might think. That doesn't work. Like,

"Hey, bro, why did you even bother saving my life if you're going to treat me like I don't exist?"

That was my perception of God for years. Yes, God sent Jesus to die for my sins. Jesus saved my eternal soul. But, I reasoned, the rescue was obligatory. God promised that those who believe in His Son will have eternal life. But God must look at me, shrug, and say, "Well I kept my promise to rescue you. Now go stand in that heavenly corner in the back while the beautiful people worship in the front row."

How wrong I was. There are no back rows and no time-out corners in heaven. God makes his forgiveness available to anyone. And His rescue plan is the best of our spiritual blessings. Why? Out of God's forgiveness many of His other spiritual blessings flow freely, like His goodness, faithfulness, peace, and joy.

How far does God's forgiveness extend? It's like a huge debt you owe that has the word *canceled* stamped across the creditor's note. Trying to "make it up" to God is irrelevant, because anything you owe has already been paid in full. There is no end to His giving. No day in sight where we cannot claim His favor.

The Bible uses two different Greek words for our English word *forgiveness*. Older translations render the second word as *remission*. Today, we use *remission* to describe a disease that has gone dormant. But originally, *remission* described something that is totally pushed away, never to be brought up again. Imagine all your actions and behaviors that defied God's ways piled in one big box. When you tell God you want to turn your life around and accept the salvation found only through His son, Jesus, God pushes that box into oblivion and stretches out His arms to you.

It's gone.

What utter relief. Thankfulness should wash over us like a cool rain dispelling the heat of a summer day. But maybe it doesn't. Your head knows of God's forgiveness, but your heart doesn't feel anything.

I'd like to suggest four possible reasons why gratitude for God's forgiveness may not come easy:

1. *Gratitude means admitting I've sinned.* You've lived a decent life. Everyone makes mistakes—what's the big deal? The big deal is that all of us have chosen to live according to our rules, not God's. Every single one of us. No one is exempt. "All have sinned and fall short of the glory of God" (Romans 3:23). Our choices shove God aside and we make it clear we don't want Him or anyone else to tell us we're doing wrong.

2. *Gratitude means admitting my sin was worth the death of Christ.* You may think your wrong choices aren't as bad as the actions of others, so can't God say, "Let's forget it and move on"? Someone has to recoup the cost of any outstanding debt. If you fail to pay what you owe for a mortgage or student loan, either your creditor or a third party still has to pay it off. That's what Jesus did. He paid what you owed God. If God let the moment go, He would no longer be a fair or just God.

3. *Gratitude means I'll need to forgive others.* Yes, it does. If God has forgiven you, He has also forgiven the person who offended both you and Him. And if you are working toward becoming like Jesus, He asks you to demonstrate His forgiveness so your offender will see what God's forgiveness looks like. When you don't forgive, you put yourself in the place of a judgmental god, and you deny the other person the saving grace of Jesus.

I know that's hard, my friend. Let's take it step by step. I predict that if you first grow in gratitude for God's forgiveness for you, forgiving others will come easier.

One last reason.

4. *I don't deserve God's forgiveness.* Maybe you are where I was. So I ask you what I asked myself: What makes you worse than anyone else? God offers forgiveness to all who call on His name, no matter what's in the past.

What would convince Jason that Bill had forgiven him? Let's rewrite the ending of our fictional story. Imagine that after Bill saved Jason's life and even paid Jason's medical bills, he went back to his yard, dug up that ruined garden plot, bricked it over, and added a fire pit and lawn furniture. Then he invited Jason for dinner.

God's gift of forgiveness saved us from our own destruction. He paid the cost for our healing and oversees our recovery from the consequences of our sin. When He comes again, He'll remove all the damage sin did to us. And He'll invite us to eat with Him in His backyard, His arms open wide in welcome.

That's forgiveness.

GRATITUDE PROMPT

Pray this with me: "Oh God, thank you for pushing aside the obstacle of my old self so nothing can get in the way of your love for me. In Jesus's name and through His life sacrifice, Amen."

32

God's Faithfulness

I will sing of the LORD's great love forever;
with my mouth I will make your faithfulness known
through all generations.

PSALM 89:1

Impatience is one of my top ten vices. I inwardly become ir-
ritated when someone is late, does a no-show, or fails to follow
through on a careless promise.

Are you with me?

Three facts remind me to calm down. First, unreliability is
part of the human condition. Second, I've had plenty of moments when I've forgotten the promises I've made or failed for
whatever reason to keep my word. Finally, the fickleness of fallible humans highlights God's faithfulness. While people will let
us down, God has a perfect record for following through on the
promises He's made.

Believing that God will always keep His promises is difficult
for some of us. We wrestle with the fallout of a father who ditched
his family and didn't leave a forwarding address. Or the marriage
partner who failed to keep the "till death do us part" part. Or a
teenage group who tells your daughter they are her best friends,
then intentionally don't invite her to their private cast party after

the spring musical. Even a friend's legitimate unavailability at a time when you need her support can leave you feeling adrift. You're uncertain it's safe to trust anyone.

In moments like those, I've learned to thank God for His faithfulness rather than stew about my friends' forgetfulness.

What makes God's faithfulness trustworthy?

God does keep His promises. When you read the Bible from beginning to end, pay attention to the times God says, "I will." Then notice when God fulfills that particular "I will." God never reneges. He fulfills every single promise. He doesn't change His mind, come up with a better plan, become too busy, or forget what He said.

The prophecies of the Old Testament are God's promises to the Jews of a better system than the Law and a preview of His plans for the salvation of the world. Every prophecy about the coming Messiah was fulfilled in Jesus Christ. Humanly speaking, that's impossible.

Faithfulness does not denote instant results. God may not fulfill his promises right away. The first hint of God's promise to send a Savior occurred in the garden of Eden. It was probably four thousand years before Jesus came to earth. That sounds like God was slow on the uptake, but the delay adds strength to His promise. He didn't forget. The long interval showed that God was carefully working out His plan, waiting until the perfect moment to reveal the ultimate answer.

God will never abandon us. Others may leave us, even those who ought to know better and who, by their very blood that now courses through our veins, should love us but don't. God knows better and loves us more. We may not feel His presence, but He is with us, and He has promised never to turn His back on us (Hebrews 13:5). God is "a father to the fatherless, a defender of widows" (Psalm 68:5). He is the best possible father anyone can ever have.

God is consistent in His kindness. Has anyone ever done a kind act for you, then a week later criticized you or taken advantage of you? It hurts, doesn't it? It's the worst of betrayals. I wonder if Jesus felt grief and hurt when Judas, one of His own disciples, turned Him over to the authorities to be crucified.

God will never betray us. He is faithfully kind. He'll provide for you today and then tomorrow. As long as you have need, He'll keep showing up. Even the best of caregivers needs a break, but God never grows weary or needs a nap.

We won't notice the full extent of God's persistent kindness until the end of our lives, when we will then see the golden thread of His faithfulness running through everything that happened to us. The patriarch Jacob, Abraham's grandson, experienced that. When his twin brother, Esau, sought revenge for Jacob's deception of their father, Jacob left his home, running for his life with only his staff in his hand. Twenty years later, he returned home with wives, children, and possessions. He knew and acknowledged that God's faithfulness and kindness had led him to this point (Genesis 32:10).

God will never give up on you. We may waver in our faithfulness to Him. We may break our promises to show up to meet with Him or be inconsistent in our forgiveness of others, our generosity, or our moral choices. How assuring that one screw-up from us will not make God throw up His hands and say, "Forget it. You're not worth it." His patience with us is as broad and long as His faithfulness. His unfailing love compels Him to keep working with us, giving us second chances and inviting us to come home to Him. Only when we have outright defied Him and turned our backs solidly away from our faith will He reluctantly let us go. He will not force us to love Him, but whatever we do will never change His love for us.

I'm learning to use the betrayal, empty promises, and forgetfulness of friends as a life prompt. In those moments, instead of fretting over the let-down, I'm starting to bow my head and thank God for His faithfulness. For no matter how undependable other people might be, you and I can always rely on God to stay with us through the worst of life and not quit until the job of getting us to heaven is finally done.

GRATITUDE PROMPT

At the end of today, recount how God has shown His faithfulness to you throughout the day. Thank God for His faithfulness to you.

33

God's Goodness

I remain confident of this:
I will see the goodness of the LORD
in the land of the living.
PSALM 27:13

When it snows in the Desert Southwest, adults and children spill outside to snap photos, catch snowflakes on fingertips, and laugh at fist-sized snowmen. We do it because the snow will be gone by that afternoon, and we celebrate while we can.

After one unusual storm that draped snow from mountain peaks to valley floors, my husband and I took a drive into the foothills to catch a closer view. Snow lay like woolen caps on the tops of the mighty saguaro cacti and etched designs into canyon crevices. It was breathtakingly beautiful. I thought, "Oh, God is so good!"

The saguaro and the snow might not agree.

"What's good about a bowl of cold, wet snow on top of my head?" the saguaro could ask.

"Ha!" the snow might respond. "I can think of better landing pads than spiney needles."

Silly, I know. But how many times do we react with "God is good all the time!" only when life is going our way? When life is a little chilly or thorny, we fall silent or mutter the words with subdued smiles and averted eyes.

God is good all the time. His intentions and actions are good, even when life screams otherwise. We may not understand what is happening, but we can still thank God for His goodness.

The biblical word for goodness has a two-sided meaning. It often plays duets with the word *kindness* in the Bible, and it also means doing what is morally right and beneficial. From a human perspective, we may not think God is being so nice. We're tempted to question the morality and wisdom of His choices. But God, in His perfect holiness, knows the best blend of kindness and morality.

Those in Jesus's day loved His miracle of feeding five thousand families with a boy's lunch (John 6:1–14). But other Jews didn't appreciate His action of turning over the business booths at the temple, scattering money and products every which way (Mark 11:15–18). As readers of the New Testament, we see Jesus's action at the temple as a good thing. He was trying to remove cheaters and greedy businessmen in order to restore the temple to a place of prayer and worship.

My daughter told my grandson to put away his toy cars before heading for bed. Moms know toy cleanup is respectful to other people, keeps everyone safe, and is a good life habit to develop. But from a two-year-old's perspective, it messes with playtime. And whoever heard of a broken toe from Matchbox cars? Mom is not being good or kind in her expectations!

As children grow older, they understand how Mom had the better idea. And when we take a closer look at God's character and motivations, we'll see God's goodness in even our not-so-fun times too.

God sees the bigger picture. We see snow on our sidewalks; God sees snowmelt that replenishes the water table. Our tiny life moment is one small puzzle piece that fits into the overall expanse of everything happening in the world. We are limited.

God is unlimited. He will do what is best for everyone, even if it is momentarily unpleasant for a few of us.

God is the absence of evil. He has no hidden agendas, no selfish motives, and no sadistic intent to harm us. He is holy and without any kind of sin. By his very God-nature, He exudes goodness. He will always do what is right.

God wants what is best for us. He loves us. He would not do anything to intentionally harm us long term. His love and concern for us is stronger and more lavish than the love of the best of parents.

How can a good God allow bad, even evil things to happen? I've said it before—we live in a fallen world. The bad that happens stems from our own poor choices, the fallout from the choices of others, or the overall systemic implosion of our world. We caused it, not God. But that begs the question, Why does God allow it?

If God let us do whatever we wanted without consequence to ourselves or others, we would become moral monsters, never learning the difference between righteousness and lawlessness. God would no longer be a just God. While it grieves our Lord to see His children suffer, He must allow His children to make their own choices. But through His goodness, God can and will take the broken pieces of life as it was not meant to be and, with our permission and cooperation, renew and restore us.

Disney dreams don't always come true. At some point—midlife and, sadly, sometimes as early as childhood—hard events smack us in the face with the reality that life was not supposed to be this way. But here we are.

God is still good. He still has good intentions, and He wants the best for us; in fact, He will do whatever is necessary to draw us close so we can catch glimpses of His goodness tucked into the canyon crevices of our lives. Because He sees the expanse of human history, will never do what is harmful or wrong, and wants only what is beneficial for us, He gives us reason to say, "God is good," no matter how life situations turn out.

Even with tears running down your face, you can say, "God is good. All the time." Because He is.

GRATITUDE PROMPT

What is happening in your life that you would call good? That you would call bad? Think of each situation, and then say, "God is good. All the time." Thank God for His righteousness and kindness that encompass the blessing of His goodness.

34

God's Unfailing Love

God demonstrates his own love for us in this:
While we were still sinners, Christ died for us.

ROMANS 5:8

"Will you still love me in morning's light?"
Hit the search bar in your memory browser to the last wedding you attended. Picture the happy couple. All brides are beautiful, so they say, and the grooms aren't so bad themselves. The photos catch us at our physical and emotional best.

Then comes the morning. Disheveled hair, no makeup, red eyes from too much of too much over the last several months of wedding prep—and a bride internalizes the stereotypical question: Will he love me as I am?

Of more prolonged insecurity is the unspoken question: Will you still love me if something happens to cause permanent disfigurement? Stories of spouses walking into a hospital room after a horrific accident and then taking the shortest route to the nearest exit, never to return, haunt us. We ask those nagging questions: Will you see beyond the scars to the person I still am and hope to reclaim? Even if I caused my own grief that led you to become mired in the fallout, will you love me back to wholeness?

God did and does, and God will continue to love you. His love lasts forever, unmarred by our circumstances or poor choices.

God's love is different than what the world knows as love. He loves what He created. He cherishes the human beings He made to be replicas of himself. How could He possibly cast away what He loves?

He is determined to love us no matter how clumsy and fickle we are in our efforts to reach back toward Him. He made the commitment even before creation to love us unconditionally. He'll hang in there with us, guiding us, protecting us, and working with us to restore and transform us back into His image. His love is stronger than any umbilical cord and closer than any parent-child relationship. Nothing this world does to discredit or destroy us will keep Him from loving us. God's love for you and me is unfailing, everlasting, consistent, and lavish.

The New Testament Greek word for this kind of love is *agape*. It is a love that wants the best for another, an intense desire to do what needs to be done for the good of the other person. While selfish intents might blemish our love for another, or someone else's lack of love for us might disable our own ability to return love, God's love never stops, never falters, and never ends. I like the newer English translations of the Old Testament word for God's kind of love—"unfailing love." God's love really will never fail. No matter what happens to you, how others fail to love you, or how the world discards you and tries to convince you that you are worthless, God still loves you.

How can you know?

God loved you enough for Jesus to die for you.

God wanted you to come back to Him so you can enjoy the kind of relationship He intended for the two of you to have. He chose to do whatever was necessary to make that happen. If there had been an easier way, He would have done it. There was no other way. As we've discovered earlier, our sin and rebellion separated us from God, and someone had to pay off the debt. In fact, Christ died while we were still sinners, before we made any attempt to know him (Romans 5:8).

I can't take it in.

Our world has trained us well. We have to be loveable to be worthy of love. We're supposed to be beautiful or at least decently attractive. No physical flaws or disabilities, or at least have an acute mind and charming personality to offset the ugliness. We're supposed to be pleasant company, interesting to talk to, and socially appropriate. We shouldn't be selfish, arrogant, or intentionally harmful to others. Then we're worth loving.

Not in God's social framework.

How can we make ourselves more attractive, pleasant, or good so God will love us more? What can we do to earn this level of love?

Nothing.

God already loves us lavishly (1 John 3:1). He's already gone the distance in expressing His love for us. He cannot possibly love us any more than He does because He already fully, unconditionally, unfailingly loves us.

Isn't that a fantastic feeling? God's love deserves to be at the top of our list of spiritual blessings. Whenever you feel like no one cares what happens to you, there is someone who does love you, no matter who you are or what you've done. You are loved, and that love will never go away.

Tell the Lord "Thank you!" with a smile on your face and a glint in your eye. "Thank you, God, for loving me." Say it out of your brokenness and grief. "Thank you, God, for loving me." Repeat it often. Say it with every prayer. Open each prayer with those precious words: "Thank you, God, for loving me."

Because He does.

GRATITUDE PROMPT

Write these words on an index card or sticky note: Thank you God for loving me. Place the note where you will see it often. Whenever you glance at the note, say the words out loud.

35

Justice

I will sing of your love and justice;
to you, Lord, I will sing praise.
Psalm 101:1

M y seventh-grade language arts class unit on Greek my-
thology confused me. As a new Christian, I wondered
how anyone could believe in Zeus, the head god of the Greek
pantheon, as a god. For one thing, if he was supposedly immortal, why didn't anyone believe in him anymore? Second,
how could an immortal god be so immoral? The stories depicted
him as nothing more than a superhero, and a capricious one
at that. Zeus may have dispensed justice, but he also used his
power and authority to seduce goddesses and earthly women,
retaliating against anyone who crossed him. He sounded more
like a spoiled child.

If he were truly a god, my young mind reasoned, wouldn't he
judge fairly without bringing in his own selfish desires?

Imagine the chaos if the universe was governed by an impulsive,
inconsistent being like Zeus. It isn't enough for a god to be all-
powerful; he must also be all-wise, all-knowing, always consistent,
and perfectly pure. Otherwise, how could we possibly trust him?
We need a God who is just.

What *is* justice?

Since the New Testament was written in Greek, being the word nerd that I am, I checked the etymology of the word the Bible uses for "justice." To my surprise the Greek word *dikaios* translates as both "righteous" and "just." A just God will always do what is morally right. He will always make the right choices and judge fairly. He will deal with those who choose to act immorally and won't play favorites, punishing some but not others.

Our human natures crave the structure of justice. Something deep within us glitches when the lines between right and wrong blur. Think of the outcry when one felon receives an extended jail term while another gets only a probation period for the same crime. God is not just, some might say. Look at all the evil people freely circulating in our world. Look how evil goes unpunished. Look how bad people rake up riches for themselves and good people suffer. You call that just?

The poet Asaph would agree. "I envied the arrogant when I saw the prosperity of the wicked," he wrote in Psalm 73:3. What kind of justice is it, he asked, when the wicked have no struggles, health issues, or problems common to the ordinary nobody (vv. 4–5)? In his struggle to understand, Asaph later says that he inquired of God and learned that God would not slack in his eternal judgment against wicked people (vv. 18–20).

If there is a disparity between who God is and what we see on earth, the problem is in our understanding of how God works, not that He is unjust. And it's acceptable to say, "God, I don't get it. Explain to me how your justice works."

Abraham did that. When God shared his plan to destroy the cities of Sodom and Gomorrah in Genesis 18:16–33, Abraham had questions. Would a just God destroy the innocent along with the wicked? "Will not the Judge of all the earth do right?" (v. 25). God's choices can be confusing. We want him to get rid of evildoers, with no consequences to the ones we would call innocent. And our standards of justice insist that God not delay His judgment or sentence of punishment. We want justice *now*.

But God's wisdom and mercy determine the best time for his execution of justice. Jesus's parable of the wheat and weeds predict the unintended consequences of rooting up evil too soon (Matthew 13:24–30). God allows evil to come to its full measure as He did with the Amorites (Genesis 15:16). And God gives evildoers every chance to repent, for in his mercy, God doesn't want any of us to eternally perish (2 Peter 3:9).

It is acceptable to struggle with the reality of unrequited evil. But to be fair to God, we need to start with respect for His justice and righteousness and then also admit that He knows what is best, far more than we do. Even after we've asked questions that seem to bring up only more questions, we'll need to take a pause break and simply say, "Thank you." Thanks that God knows what is right, He knows how to handle it, and His far-reaching foresight knows how everything will be handled in the end.

David expressed it well: "Do not fret because of those who are evil or be envious of those who do wrong; for like the grass they will soon wither, like green plants they will soon die away" (Psalm 37:1–2). Justice may not happen as quickly as we like, but God has promised He will deal with evil—in the right way, at the right time, and with the right amount of righteousness and love. We can join David in saying, "I will sing of your love and justice; to you, LORD, I will sing praise."

I might question God's time frames and methods in dealing with unfair life situations and worldwide wickedness, but He does a much better job at dispensing justice than I ever could. In fact, He does the best job because He is God, and God is just and righteous. All the time.

For that, I am thankful.

GRATITUDE PROMPT

Name a corrupt situation in the news or within your life circle that distresses you. Thank God for His ultimate justice—that He knows about the situation and will make everything right in the end.

36

Righteousness

In the gospel the righteousness of God is revealed—a
righteousness that is by faith from first to last, just as
it is written: "The righteous will live by faith."

ROMANS 1:17

Have you noticed a business whose management model made
work harder than it needed to be? Have you ever done a
particular tedious task for years only to discover there was an easier
way that could have saved you loads of time, tears, and money?

I treated my relationship with Jesus that way for over a decade.
Yes, accepting Jesus as Savior made me righteous, or "right with
God," but I wanted to be more right. So I did all the external
things I thought God would like. Read the Bible. Pray. Serve the
church and others. Make moral choices. All those are good things,
but I still felt empty, like I hadn't quite received God's acceptance.

Most religions throughout human history base their tenets on
external acts of righteousness. To get God's or the gods' approval,
you have to accomplish a certain list of dos and don'ts. Make
sacrifices. Attend group gatherings. Give to the less fortunate.
Control your physical passions. Individually, we add myriads of
personal expectations as we attempt to reach toward becoming
more perfectly acceptable to a righteous and holy God. Realizing

we're not perfect, we boil it down to a few expectations. If we do certain things, we should be good with God. Right? He's a loving, forgiving God, right? Somehow, our fingers never quite touch.

Reaching God seems insurmountable.

But there is another way to reach our righteous God. It's called faith.

God bases His standards for righteousness on our faith and trust in Him, not on robotic movement through a list of rituals. A faith-based system of righteousness makes more sense. It looks at the internal motivations of the heart rather than a duty-bound obligation that could lead us to resent what we view as an unreachable God.

Abram (who later became known as Abraham) in the Old Testament discovered this streamlined approach to righteousness. God had made several impossible-sounding promises to this rather ordinary man. God would lead Abram to a new land. Abraham's descendants would inherit that land. All people on earth would be blessed through him (Genesis 12:1–3).

There was one big hitch: Abraham had no children. It was too late now, for Abraham and his wife, Sarah, were too old to have children. Surely there was a workaround. Maybe the promised children were figurative or not blood related. But no, God would give him a son of his very own that would put this plan in motion. God took Abraham outside one evening. "'Look up at the sky and count the stars—if indeed you can count them.' Then he said to him, 'So shall your offspring be'" (Genesis 15:5).

The next verse was my big aha moment: "Abram believed the LORD and he credited it to him as righteousness" (v. 6). Abraham accepted that, as impossible as it sounded, God would do what He promised. God, in turn, accepted Abraham's show of faith as an act of righteousness. In their teaching about the connection of faith to our being right with God, the writings of Paul and James in the New Testament both refer to the crucial role of Abraham's faith (Romans 4:3; Galatians 3:6; James 2:23). When God assesses our relationship with Him, He looks at our faith-based response to His promises. He counts faith as a righteous act.

How does that work?

I used to measure my worth to God by the work I did each day, especially work done in His name. It was exhausting and self-defeating because all the things I hadn't done stared me in the face at end of day.

Then I started looking at life from the perspective of faith. How had I activated my faith in God that day? What was my attitude and motivation for action? Were my choices motivated by love for God and a trust in His wisdom and power or by my own desire to look good to God and everyone else?

When I prayed, had I shown my confidence in God's interest, willingness, and power to answer simply by sharing my needs with Him? When I let go of my to-do list to help someone in trouble, did I do it out of obligation and frustration—or did I quietly agree with God about His priorities for my life and entrust the management of my hours to Him? Had I told someone about the goodness of God? While that seems like an action, that came from a place of faith too, for it demonstrated my willingness to turn the spotlight away from how accomplished I was to what I believed about God's greatness.

God's structure for righteousness gets better. As we discovered earlier, we cannot attain perfection on our own, and we can't coexist with the pure, holy, righteous God because of our unrighteousness. But God sent Jesus to cover the perfection gap between God and us. Jesus's death entitles me to a right relationship with God. God no longer looks at my own righteous activity or lack of it, but on Jesus's righteousness that is not my own. "I have been crucified with Christ and I no longer live, but Christ lives in me" (Galatians 2:20).

All God asks is that we accept His model of righteousness. Accepting Jesus's sacrifice really is an easier way, the best way. The only way.

You and I can thank God that He knows what is right and that what He does will always be right. We can also thank Him that He makes it possible for us to know and do what is right too, that we can be righteous like Him. He bases our righteousness not on our own perfection or lack of it, but on our faith and confidence in the promises He made and His fulfillment of them through Jesus.

GRATITUDE PROMPT

How have today's life choices flowed out of your faith in God? Thank God for His system of righteousness, that He bases His approval of you not on what you do but on your faith in what He and His Son Jesus have done for you.

37

Grace

Thanks be to God for his indescribable gift!
2 CORINTHIANS 9:15

B ack in the day when photos were in the form of prints or slides projected on a pulldown screen, my family often gathered for family slide shows. My aunt and uncle loved to travel, and we equally loved their travelogues. Uncle Eldon was a particularly adept storyteller, and I sat enthralled by his narratives.

Uncle Eldon was also a big tease. He'd pick on me, I'd get indignant, and he'd laugh. I went back for more because I loved his laugh and the attention. But one day I went too far. Piqued by something he'd said, I jumped up in mock irritation, careless about my movements. My arm shot out and tore the edge of the projection screen.

I froze in horror. What would my parents say? Unknown to our extended family, my stepfather often became irate at the smallest infraction. I figured I'd be expected to pay somehow for the damage of that beautiful screen.

"How much will that cost to replace?" I asked in a small voice.

Uncle Eldon lifted his hand. "It's all right." And he smiled that grin I loved.

I never heard another word about that ripped screen. The next time we came to their house, I looked. There was no rip, and I couldn't tell whether it was a new screen. I didn't dare ask. It seemed inappropriate. It was over.

That, my friend, is grace.

Compared to the apostle Paul, my screen demolition was child's play. Before he encountered Jesus, Paul had a personal vendetta to destroy Christians. No, he didn't shove in the sword or drive the nails, but he was complicit in the plot to round them up and get them gone. In Paul's mad dash toward vengeance, he opposed the very plan God had set in motion and became a murderer in the process.

Paul didn't merit one shred of mercy. He deserved the worst of punishments. He said so himself (1 Corinthians 15:9). Yes, you may think he should be saved because God's grace is available to all, but give him the job of carrying the gospel message to the rest of the known world and let him write a third of the New Testament? That's way more than that dude deserved.

Yet Jesus met him on the road to Damascus, proved His identity as the Son of God, and then drew Paul into His circle of influencers (Acts 9:15). The past—his religious zeal gone sour—was no longer an issue. Never held against him again. Such a non-issue that we often forget what Paul once was. The only one who brought up the matter after Paul's conversion was Paul himself—and that was only in the context of his testimony.

That grace enveloped Paul for the rest of his life. I wonder if he had grace at the forefront of his mind when he praised God for blessing us "in the heavenly realms with every spiritual blessing in Christ" (Ephesians 1:3), a blessing that God had planned for us since before creation. Paul's personal encounter with Jesus validated the words he spoke in one of his other letters: "There is now no condemnation for those who are in Christ Jesus" (Romans 8:1).

We all deserve the punishment of death because we have also rebelled against God. But Jesus relinquished His heavenly role, came to earth in human form, and gave himself up to be put to death as a substitute for the rest of us.

It's tough to wrap our brains around the idea that someone died for us. Why did God have to be that extreme to get us to return to Him? Pride makes us wonder, "Was I really that bad? Do I honestly want someone to do something that big for me? Surely I can take care of this myself."

The truth is, even if I want to admit I need to get back to God, there's nothing I can do on my own to make things perfectly right. What if, after I'd torn the screen, I had gone home and shook out the dimes and quarters from my piggy bank and then, each week, handed Uncle Eldon a fistful of coins, hoping to pay for that ripped screen? I think I would have made my uncle cry. It would have been clear I didn't understand what "it's all right" meant.

Even the most righteous person among us falls short of God's glory and holiness. If we never did anything wrong for the rest of our lives, we would still bear the stain of sin from what we've done in the past. But no worries! Jesus has already paid the debt to set us free and then has invited us to be partners with Him in His work, putting all the resources of His kingdom at our disposal. No matter what we've done in the past, if we accept what He's done for us, we are free.

I'm overwhelmed. How do I agree to receive what I don't deserve?

God asks that we simply accept the gift of His grace. Accept through belief that Jesus did this for us, not because we deserve it but because we need it.

I'm relieved Uncle Eldon said those beautiful words, "It's all right." I'm relieved I didn't have to pay for a projection screen nickel by nickel. Better yet, his in-the-flesh gift of grace—refusing to let my carelessness get in the way of my relationship with him, no matter what it cost him—gave me a concrete example of the meaning of grace.

I can respond to God the same way I reacted to Uncle Eldon.

I can trust the generosity of the gift, believe His good will and love for me, and treat Him like I believe He loves me.

GRATITUDE PROMPT

How has someone's act of grace helped you understand the grace of God? Thank God for loving you enough to extend His grace and mercy to you.

38

Peace

The peace of God, which transcends all understanding,
will guard your hearts and your minds in Christ Jesus.

PHILIPPIANS 4:7

I often wake up around 4:30 a.m. from dry eyes or a stuffy nose. Almost as often, I stay awake because of what my husband and I call "busy brain." Problem solving, that's what it is. The brain kicks in with the events of the previous day, and in the quiet of early morning, my mind tries to sort out life and mentally fix everything.

I haven't fooled God one bit. Busy brain is a fancy word for worry. And worry is hard work. By 6:00 a.m., I'm exhausted because my worry brain has run serpentine laps around situations over which I have little control.

In one season of a long list of concerns, I finally listened to my own advice that I've presented to my family countless times: "Have you prayed about it?" Ever the organizer, I wrote the list on my whiteboard, surrendering each issue to the Lord's care before I started my workday. That helped. Somewhat. I was still waking up, and the issues remained unresolved.

Then I remembered my friend Stephen's experience of lacing

gratitude into his prayer concerns. Were God's gifts and blessings embedded within each of my concerns?

I couldn't make it through the second item on my list before a smile creased my face and my shoulder muscles relaxed. I found myself thanking God for the people each problem represented: good, loving people who loved their Lord and worked with me to make God's work a reality. I thanked God for the possibilities each challenge represented. All the problems on my list were good problems, exciting problems. They were just not moving as fast or as obviously as I wanted. The situations reminded me how God had provided for me in the past and how He was the one who had opened the doors of possibility. If He had done it before, wouldn't He be faithful to do it again?

If I could describe my feelings by the end of that gratitude session in one word, it would be peace. And Paul, speaking God's wisdom, would agree. "The peace of God, which transcends all understanding, will guard your hearts and your minds in Christ Jesus."

Gratitude and peace have a symbiotic relationship with each other. We experience peace when we combine thanks with our petitions. Before, my prayers were best buddies with worry. It was hard to tell where worry ended and prayer began. My prayers ricocheted between a desperate "Help me" and a defiant "You've got to do something." But when gratitude replaced worry, my words softened. I wasn't fighting God any longer or chafing at His timetable. My gratitude showed I valued what He had done before and trusted what He would do again. A peace that made no sense in human terms encircled my thinking, and that list on my white board no longer seemed as desperate. My prayers turned to an attitude of "Here's what I'd like to see happen, Lord. However you choose to handle it, I'm cool. I'm confident you will do exactly what needs to be done."

Peace is the absence of strife. Peace finds agreement and solidarity with another. Peace is a gift and outgrowth of our trusting relationship with God.

Moments when senseless tragedy taunts any semblance of peace will still happen. Everything within us might strain against the unfairness, the inexplicable suffering, and the lack of resolution. We will cry out for mercy, justice, and explanation. "May God give you peace," those watching us will say, and we will want to spit back, "There is no peace. This is so very wrong."

But we only find peace when we surrender the situation fully to God, thanking Him for knowing what He is doing and acknowledging that we're willing to let Him work His plan. Like trusting the pilot who has the skill, instruments, and control tower directions to guide a plane through thick fog, we can relax because we know God is at our life's helm, and He will bring us safety through the worst of storms.

When we center on His power and love and trust Him to do what's best, He will give us perfect peace (Isaiah 26:3), a peace that the world can't begin to fathom. Others will look at us and wonder, "Aren't you nervous? Afraid? Shouldn't you be doing something?" No. God's got this. I can go on. I can relax. I can go back to sleep at 4:30 in the morning because I'm not questioning how my CEO is managing the affairs of my life.

He truly has given me His peace.

GRATITUDE PROMPT

What is on your worry list? Thank God that He is in control and that He offers you the gift of His peace that will soften the tension you feel as you learn to trust His best plans for you.

39

Holy Spirit

I will ask the Father, and he will give you another
advocate to help you and be with you forever.

JOHN 14:16

I have weak moments when I hear about a friend's family vacation to Europe, anniversary celebration in Hawaii, evening
out at an upscale restaurant, or new furniture purchase. It must
be nice, I say to myself.

As we've discovered, when a have-not spirit threatens to suck
the joy from our day, we Christ followers have a ticker tape list
of spiritual blessings at our constant disposal. Yet God gives us
another astonishing gift far more valuable than new furniture,
and that will take us to places far more exciting than Hawaii. God
puts a piece of himself, the Holy Spirit, inside us.

What does it mean to have the gift of the Holy Spirit? Certain
groups within the last century have aimed a narrow beam on what
the Holy Spirit does. Yet the work of the Holy Spirit is more
expansive than merely an aid to personal and public worship.
Perhaps we've relegated the Holy Spirit to the role of worship
leader because to consider the broader scope of who He is and
what He does would be overwhelming.

I dare you to be overwhelmed.

It's incredible enough that God has promised to be with us. The creator and ruler of the universe says He will be with us through anything we face. Yet Jesus promised something more. When we come to saving faith in Christ and are baptized into the name of Jesus, God gives us His Spirit to live inside us (Acts 2:38).

God. Living within us. Paul writes, "Now to him who is able to do immeasurably more than all we ask or imagine, according to his power that is at work within us . . ." (Ephesians 3:20). And later he says, "It is God who works in you to will and to act in order to fulfill his good pleasure" (Philippians 2:13).

All those character traits that represent the nature of God— they're what God puts inside of you. He will change you from who you used to be to who He is. As His Spirit takes up residence in your life, He makes available to you all the resources of heaven. God wants to work through you to bring His message of grace, love, peace, and hope to the world He longs to reclaim, and He'll resource you to be His ambassador.

How does that work in everyday life?

When you speak on His behalf, He'll work with you to craft the words He wants said (Luke 12:11–12).

When you need reassurance, encouragement, wisdom in living obediently, or comfort, He'll bring the words of the Bible to your mind, even if it's a verse you haven't read or thought of for several years (John 14:26).

The struggle and lure of sin will no longer be as strong, and you'll think of God-honoring alternative choices, for the Spirit of Christ entwined with your spirit prioritizes a different agenda than the earthbound old you (Galatians 2:20).

God's alternate way of life will transform you in the form of a list of behaviors called the fruit of the spirit (Galatians 5:22–23).

The Holy Spirit will empower you to do things you've never done before, never gone to school to learn, and may seem humanly impossible (Ephesians 3:20–21).

You will never be alone again. God will partner with you in everything you do (John 14:16).

There's one more blessing of Holy Spirit indwelling. You may not feel the difference or see an outward sign of this when you first welcome Jesus into your life. But it's a difference the spiritual world takes note of. By giving the Holy Spirit to you, God puts a seal on you that marks you as His (Ephesians 1:13). It's like God's personal QR code: "This one belongs to me." Forever, God has claimed you as part of His family, and no one can take you away from the Lord you love.

The Holy Spirit is an incredible blessing, one that deserves far more than a robotic thank-you. A business partnership works best if the two associates are in continual communication with each other. In the same way, we'll appreciate the full extent of the Holy Spirit's indwelling when we invite Him to be an active part of our daily equation instead of ignoring or forgetting about His presence. Our use of God's gift proclaims our gratitude.

God's Spirit lives in you. He invites you to share every moment of your life with Him. Thank Him when He plants a Scripture in the forefront of your mind, guides you to the right moment to accomplish His will for you, or puts words in your mouth that cannot be from any other source but Him. And on the days you don't feel anything, simply thank Him that His invisible label is on your soul and that all of heaven knows you belong to Christ.

GRATITUDE PROMPT

How have you seen the Holy Spirit working in your life in the past week? Thank God that He lives within you and wants to use you in His kingdom work.

40

Hope

May the God of hope fill you with all joy and
peace as you trust in him, so that you may overflow
with hope by the power of the Holy Spirit.

ROMANS 15:13

With patient good humor, my family and close friends put up with my jokes about their letting me drive. Since I have never driven in my life, we all know I'm not serious. If I offer to drive, they treat it like a comedic straight line and rise to the challenge of countering with an appropriate comeback.

"Let me check my insurance coverage."

"Sure! But I'll find a ride with someone else."

"I want to go to heaven, but not today."

Going to heaven wouldn't bother me. For when I reach heaven, then I'll be able to see as fully as Jesus sees me. That's the hope that lives within me.

I sometimes forget, when I make one of my outrageous comments, that my audience may not know I don't drive. One morning, on our way home from visiting our daughter, my husband and I headed toward the motel parking lot. Two motorcyclists stood next to our car, making final adjustments to their helmets and packing their sidecar.

I paused to admire their bikes. They were awesome. We chatted a bit about their trek across the country, and I concluded the conversation with a big smile and the comment, "That sounds like a lot of fun. When I get to heaven, I'm going to ride a moped."

Clueless, one biker asked, "Why not now?"

I was nice. And truthful. "I'm visually impaired, so I don't think that's going to happen. But I'm really looking forward to heaven, because when I get there, I'll be able to see to ride that moped. It will be awesome!"

The biker shifted. "Oh." And he swung his leg over the motorcycle seat.

I wish he'd been more curious. I wanted to tell him my story. My internal motor revved as I itched to give an account for the hope that was in me. I wanted to share why I'm confidently looking forward to heaven. I've had a glimpse of what better can look like, and I can't wait for more.

In heaven, all of us will have better-than-ever vision. We'll have better-than-ever of everything. Physical weaknesses, heartache, and emotional baggage will slip from our backs and hearts as we enter heaven's halls.

Am I crazy? How can I be that confident? What if the idea of an afterlife is a hoax?

One of the greatest blessings of improved eyesight is realizing that better eyesight is even possible. In the same way, Jesus showed us that a better-than-ever life was possible when He rose from the dead. He proved there could be life, glorious life, after earthly death. If He could come back to life after promising He would, isn't it plausible that He will fulfill his promise to take those of us who put our trust in Him to the place He has prepared for us (John 14:2)?

But what if Jesus hadn't come back to life?

Then, as Paul said, we are a people to be pitied (1 Corinthians 15:19). But I think I would rather have the confident hope that Jesus does offer eternal life than be a skeptic and find out at the beginning of eternity what I could have had.

Hope propels us forward. Hope offers us a glimpse of the best while we huddle in the trenches of the worst. Hope is not a hesitant and doubtful wish. It centers its anticipation on the confidence that God will keep His promises because He has always proven trustworthy before.

Hope gives us perspective during the tough seasons of life. This one moment in time might be the worst moment of our lives, but through the strength and love of the Lord we trust that the next moment or the next day will be better. Life may get worse before it gets better, but it will get better. We are convinced God will see us through, stronger and better, until the end of the heartache.

I've heard many Christ followers say, "I don't know how people make it through without hope." Hope—believing things will be better. Hope—believing to the depths of your soul that someone knows about the mess you face and can do something about it. Hope that follows you to the grave and whispers, "Hang on, beloved. Someone will meet you on the other side."

I'm grateful for God's brand of hope, for it is His hope that gives me reason to get up in the morning, put one foot in front of the other, and keep enduring through what the world wants to tell me is hopeless. I have hope because there is a God who cares personally about me and wants and has the power and authority to give me the very best heaven has to offer.

The hope God gives steers me through the worst of what life throws at me toward the best that is yet to come.

GRATITUDE PROMPT

Lift up your head from your current heartache, my friend. What, in this hour, gives you hope? Thank God for that hope. Ask the Lord to fill you with the joy and peace that come from belief in Him so you may abound in hope.

PART FIVE

Those Who Walk with Us

A cord of three strands is not quickly broken.

ECCLESIASTES 4:12

God works through people to bless us, strengthen us, and bear the burdens of life with us. Our people connections make us strong.

41

The Gift of You

Thank you for making me so wonderfully complex!
Your workmanship is marvelous—how well I know it.

PSALM 139:14 NLT

None of us is a solo act.

God surrounds each of us with a collection of people who interconnect with each other, support each other, and protect each other. Through the unique gifts and strengths of each person, we work together to make the community stronger. Family and close friends stand on either side of us. Others take their place down the line, beyond our periphery, but still influence and add their resources to our relentless march toward heaven.

You can't do life by yourself. But the rest of your sphere can't do it without you either.

You are amazing and needed.

Please, don't discount what I say. God has made you uniquely you, one of a kind, different from the rest of the twenty billion people who have taken up residence on this planet. And your uniqueness spans more than just a fingerprint.

Our DNA code offers infinite combinations of complex differences. No two human beings are alike. Even identical twins have something singular about each one. Add the layer of our mental capabilities and structure of our personalities. The parents among us will nod their heads vigorously. Isn't it amazing how two children, born from the same parents can be such opposites? My older daughter was a math and science whiz, but the younger one snapped up foreign languages. I wasn't proficient in any of those subjects, and none of us knows how to throw a basketball.

Our individual experiences add the next tier of exclusiveness. None of us have had the exact same combination of life happenings. Two people may have both been through similar situations like grief, divorce, and disabilities, but the circumstances for each person stand on their own. That doesn't need to discourage you. Don't think, "No one understands." Rather, consider that you have something singular to bring to the table. Others need to hear your voice and your perspective.

God customizes you in one more way. When you accept Christ as your Savior and Lord and are baptized into His name, you receive the gift of the Holy Spirit (Acts 2:38). And God tailors a Holy Spirit gift to fit who you are, gifting you with abilities beyond your DNA code. He equips you with skills meant for you to use for His kingdom work, to bless God's people and give witness to those who do not yet know Jesus. The spiritual gifts mentioned in Paul's letters are merely a starting point. The all-powerful God can equip you for a lifetime or for a season to do the work He has called you to do, with resources uniquely crafted to fit the person He has already created you to be.

Even your flaws, mistakes, foolish choices, and weaknesses are part of the package deal of who you are and what others need from you. Paul confides to the Corinthians how God chose to use Paul's personal weakness, which he called a "thorn in my flesh," for His glory (2 Corinthians 12:7). It was part of who Paul was.

So thank God for the gift of you.

Does that sound arrogant? It's not. Your gratitude honors the One who gave you all that is distinctly you. Appreciation for who you are pushes back the temptation to bend yourself into something that you are not in order to please someone who is not God.

That's a hard call for young and old alike. We're all under pressure to become like those around us—to dress, act, and excel in the same way. I find it amusing that, throughout multiple generations, some people defiantly strain against cultural norms, insisting they want to be their own person. Yet their choices reveal they are trying to fit in with others who are pursuing a countercultural lifestyle. I saw my daughters struggle against this in high school. When I encouraged them to take the risk of choosing the fashions they liked the best and what looked best on their body type, they retreated with dismay. Can't do that, they told me. They wouldn't fit in.

God calls us to follow Him and grow toward what He has planned for us to be, not what everyone is like. He calls us to not conform to the common pattern of the world, but to let Him transform us into His image (Romans 12:2). He invites us to be truly different and one of a kind so we singularly reflect His character.

It's scary. It's risky. We'll stand out when we might want to hide in the crowd. But the unique you is who God has planned for you to be. And if that's God's plan for you, and He does all things well, why not thank Him for who you are?

The best way to thank God for making you in such a marvelous way is to live out the pattern He intended for you. And as you live and discover His custom-made creation, you'll delight even more at the intricacies of His design. Then you'll agree with the psalmist, "Your workmanship is marvelous!"

GRATITUDE PROMPT

Write a list of traits, gifts, experiences, and weaknesses that make you uniquely you. Thank God that He has made you wonderfully complex.

42

Family

God sets the lonely in families,
he leads out the prisoners with singing;
but the rebellious live in a sun-scorched land.

PSALM 68:6

I slumped in a medical office's waiting room chair, my two-week-old baby asleep in her car carrier at my feet. We were about to consult with the third doctor of the day about the possibility of her imminent eye surgery. Although medical procedures had advanced tremendously since I first faced surgery for congenital cataracts thirty years before, I grappled with the reality that my baby had the same eye issues as I did.

You would think we should have thought about this before now. We knew my condition was genetic. We also knew that medical and educational opportunities had taken great leaps forward in the past thirty years, and the future looked much brighter for our daughter. We took the risk of bearing children because we knew through my life experience that life could be full and productive.

But reality is different than speculation. How can I be a good mother to a visually impaired child, I wondered. Raising a disabled child with courage and determination looked good on paper, but could we really pull it off as parents? And could I stand it emotionally to watch my baby go through surgery?

I felt utterly alone.

I looked across the room. My mother sat, reading a magazine. She had flown to be with us after the birth of the baby before we knew the diagnosis. Then it hit me: Mother knows. She's been there. She sat in medical waiting rooms during my own surgeries.

I was not alone. I had family. I had their faith. Even when Mother boarded her plane later that afternoon, I retained all she had taught me.

Family is the foundation of societal structure. Family is like the inner steel girding of a tall building. Whether your family is loving and supportive or contentious and estranged, they are the people who remind you most of who you are and where you came from.

As I browsed through biblical references to families, a recurring theme ran through the Old Testament. Leaders for religious and governmental positions were selected from the heads of families, the ones who represented their family in important gatherings. Thus, the family unit was the basis for raising the future leaders of the community. The family worshiped God together, as shown through Passover and other religious celebrations. God used families to pass on His words, His laws, and knowledge of who He is.

Family relationships become boot camp for our dealings with people beyond the borders of our home property. Our family unit is supposed to teach us how to stay close to each other even under duress and how to support each other through the worst of times.

When trouble strikes, whom do we most likely go to first? Our families. Once, when my husband was recovering from a torn Achilles tendon, my brother and sister-in-law came to town. I grabbed their availability to help me run errands but apologized. "Rotten way to spend your vacation," I joked.

"No!" my sister-in-law protested. "That's what families do. We help each other."

She was right. If I'd asked a friend or neighbor, I would have felt compelled to pay for their gas or take a gift. With family, we help each other out, knowing that the next time we need help, they'll be there for us.

Families understand each other, even the little quirks. It's comfortable being with family because, for the most part, you share the same values and way of doing things. Since my family has several visually impaired people in our clan, whenever we go out to eat, those with sight issues immediately claim the seats with their backs to the windows and the normally sighted people let them. It happens without one spoken word. It's a relief that I don't have to explain my need. My family knows.

Families offer comfort and support when life gets tough. When my husband lost a job, we were devastated. Both sides of the family listened, supported, and prayed. One family member drove over three hundred miles to spend a weekend pampering me and the girls with manicures, a movie, and dinner out.

You may wonder, "What family do you belong to? Mine doesn't work like that." Sadly, dysfunction has stolen God's original intent of the function of the family. Every family bears marks of betrayal and brokenness, including mine. Society would have us believe we can do without the family structure. After all, look how your family messed with you.

Your immediate family may have let you down, but that doesn't mean the family structure is a bad idea. We are all flawed and fallible. If you come from a family who didn't watch out for you, reflect on those people God brought into your life during your childhood who did love you, guided you, and gave you a structure of how to live life. It might have been and still may be an aunt, grandparent, or sibling who is your go-to person when life becomes unbearable. They are the ones who speak your language and remind you that you are not alone. They are the people with whom, when you get together, you feel like you've come home.

God was smart to create the structure of family. Children

need that safe loving environment in which to begin those first, vulnerable years of life. Aged parents need the love and comfort of those who come behind them to care for them in their final days. And if your family could have done a better job of supporting each other, you can thank God He's given you His model for the family unit within the pages of the Bible that empowers you to replicate the strong family God wants you to have.

GRATITUDE PROMPT

How has a family member blessed you in the last week? Thank God—and them—for what they have done for you.

43

Neighbors

Love your neighbor as yourself.

Luke 10:27

"Welcome home!" The voice came from the small yard adjoining our neighbor's home. "Did you have a good time?" What a nice way to come home after a week spent with my daughter's family. And the neighbor across the street made it better. "How are your grandchildren?" Someone remembered where we had gone. *Do you want to see my pictures?*

It's such a relief to have good neighbors: people who watch over our property, bring in our trash bin, pick up our mail, or retrieve unexpected packages. One neighbor brought over lunch for my convalescing husband when I was away on a speaking trip. It's comfortable to do things for them in return, like bake cookies or chase after an escaped pet.

I'm glad God has brought us into a good neighborhood. It's reassuring to see the same faces each day and relax into their routines. Their friendly greetings are a gift in themselves. We share much in common. We talk easily on a variety of topics. In many ways, they are like me, in the same socioeconomic status. They're "nice" people.

I find it easy to love my neighbors. My familiar neighbors.

The good neighbors. But, true to form, Jesus broadened the definition of the word *neighbor* when He told the parable of the Good Samaritan (Luke 10:25–37).

Robbers attacked a Jewish traveler and dumped his wounded body on the side of the road. Two religious workers, people one would expect to offer aid, passed by on the other side, not wanting to get involved. The person who did stop belonged to an ethnic group the Jews had learned to hate—the Samaritans. But this foreigner treated the man's wounds, loaded him on his donkey, took him to the nearest inn, and paid for his care.

"Which of these three do you think was a neighbor?" Jesus asked (v. 36). The obvious answer is the man who showed mercy. But this rearranges our concept of neighborliness faster than the boy down the street can shuffle our garden stones. According to Jesus, a neighbor is not necessarily the person we've shared property lines with for fifty years or the residents within in our gated community that only accepts certain kinds of people. Jesus challenges us to define a neighbor as the person we stand next to at any given moment. Being neighborly means doing those neighborly things to anyone who enters our space, no matter how different that person might be from us.

God gives perspective on how we treat those who intersect our life paths. He calls us to love our neighbors as ourselves. That means I will want the best for another person, no matter who they are or what they've become, just as I would want the best for myself. I would treat them as I would want them to treat me (6:31).

How do I love someone vastly different from me, someone from a different ethnic, political, religious, or economic background? Or, even if all those parameters are the same, a person with certain quirks and preferences that represent ways of living I would never do?

How do we love our neighbors as ourselves?

A first step is thanking God for the person you want to learn to love.

God created whoever stands next to you. He or she breaths the breath of God, the same as you. The Lord has gifted him with a unique set of abilities, personality, and experiences just as He has done for you. Yes, she has her flaws, but Christ died for her even as He died for you.

Thank God that He brought this person into your life and is teaching you about the nature of people as you engage with this individual. Thank the Lord for the chance to show him or her what His love looks like in real time.

It's easier to love the familiar and the comfortable. But God calls us to love the unbelieving, undeserving, and unfriendly, even when—especially when—it's not easy. For it is in those moments that we imitate the friendship of God.

If you wonder how you can possibly be thankful for someone who is your polar opposite and—let's be honest—rubs you the wrong way, ask God to show you how. Then find a way to act like a good Samaritan to them, and watch God build the relationship. You may have just found your next best neighbor.

GRATITUDE PROMPT

Whom have you encountered today? They are your neighbors. Thank God for the opportunities He gives you to share His love with them.

44

Church People

We always thank God for all of you and
continually mention you in our prayers.

1 Thessalonians 1:2

At times, church people drive me crazy. You too?
Quirky insistence of personal preferences. Squabbles over insignificant stuff. Well, in my mind at least. At any time, all of us have had moments when we felt our personal concern should be the most important item on the next church board meeting's agenda. Then there's the uninformed opinions and clumsy takes on doctrine. Poor life choices of some members and knee-jerk criticism from others who haven't bothered to find out all the facts.

How can we possibly thank God for the church when it's such a mess?

The apostle Paul must have struggled with that as he pondered the opening lines of his letter to the Corinthian church, a group troubled with conflict. Silly stuff like who baptized whom and who had the more essential spiritual gifts. Serious sins like incest and lawsuits against fellow believers. Doctrinal inaccuracies like misunderstandings over the role of spiritual gifts and Jesus's resurrection.

Yet Paul wrote as he did to other churches, "I always thank my God for you" (1 Corinthians 1:4). How could Paul be thankful for this group of people who had strayed from Jesus's vision for the church?

He saw their potential of what they could become, and he was confident God would be faithful in providing and protecting His people (vv. 4–8).

Too often the spotlight of social media and news sources shine on the sins and shortcomings of the church. Even church members often think first about what's wrong with the church. But I need to do the same reality check on myself that I wish others would do. Not everyone who walks in the door of a church building is a believer in Jesus Christ. Christ came to redeem the sick and lost, and that means the church is going to have those kinds of people in it.

But how do we deal with people we know are believers but who, we impatiently think, ought to know better? There are steps straight from Paul's writings that we can take to help us be thankful for the person sitting in the seat next to us.

1. My brothers and sisters in Christ are sinners saved by grace—just like me.
2. They are learning how to trust God and use the gifts He's given them—maybe at a different pace or in singular ways, but still—just like me.
3. They are growing in their understanding and ability to express biblical truths—just like me.

The church is not perfect, not by a long shot. And yes, any group of believers has the potential for infiltrators, people there for the wrong reasons or who have bought into worldly ideas or practices. Jesus and the early church warned that would happen.

The church is still beautiful. It may consist of a group of people who meet at a certain location every Sunday morning, a smaller group that gathers in a home, or a fellow Christ follower who chats with you about faith over the workplace coffeepot. The church is any group who works together to proclaim Jesus to the rest of the world and cheer each other on. Paul saw this in the church at Thessalonica. He thanked God for "your work produced by faith, your labor prompted by love, and your endurance inspired by hope in our Lord Jesus Christ" (1 Thessalonians 1:3).

During a three-year span at one of my husband's small-church ministries, we saw key leadership picked off one-by-one through major health issues. I'm not talking about common things like cancer and heart issues. These were diseases none of us had heard of before. Simple things turned into major complications. Yet as we watched this group of people walk through tragedy after tragedy, we witnessed faithful believers refuse to give up. Their strong faith and hope that God would see them through held them together. And we saw love expressed through mercy as they took care of and faithfully prayed for each other.

The next time you want to throw up your hands in frustration at what you see happening within your group of Christ followers, use Paul's three-point prayer of gratitude for the Thessalonians. How has that group lived their faith and trust in God? How have they shown love to each other and to outsiders? How have they endured through tough times because of the hope they have in Jesus?

Most of all, thank God for His grace and patience in bringing such a group of people together and helping them grow strong in their faith, love, and hope. Their work and lives may not be perfect or as far along as you would like, but when believers accept God's grace, God has something to work with, and He will be faithful in holding the church together.

GRATITUDE PROMPT

Make a list of the good things you see happening within your group of believers. How have you seen believers show their faith, love, and hope in God? Thank God for the church people He has placed around you.

45

Besties

There is a friend who sticks closer than a brother.
PROVERBS 18:24

If you have a best friend, you are blessed.

Friendship comes in various forms. Some friends are the best of the best—one who stands in our inner circle, close enough to see our stray facial hair and inner flaws yet still love us. Others could say they have a composite of friends: companions for different parts of life, all dear, but each fulfilling a different role of friendship.

Then we have friendships we could call the best of the rest. Our Christmas card list is shrinking, our closest friends have died or moved away, and we hardly trust the friends that are left because they've let us down one too many times. They'll do in a pinch, we're doing our part to be a good friend, but the relationships stay in the shallow end of the pool, too superficial to mean much of anything.

Friendship is risky because the other person may not be all we want or need them to be at any given time. Yet the best or closest friendships thrive when we are all too human. The other person accepts us as we are but raises the bar for what we can become.

The relationship strengthens from our mutual commitment to stick to each other no matter how messy life gets.

That defines the deep friendship David and Jonathan enjoyed. Scripture says that Jonathan, heir apparent to King Saul, loved David, a shepherd from a remote village, as himself (1 Samuel 18:1–2; 20:17). Jonathan shared his possessions with David, including his clothes. Letting David wear his robe meant David would now look like a king's son.

Letting someone use your favorite archery bow and burrow into your clothes hamper sounds chummy. Some have wondered if the relationship between these two men was not honorable. But as we jump from 1 Samuel 18 to chapter 20, we see that their relationship was anything but physical. They were willing to remain friends even when the rest of the world stood against one of them.

Jonathan's father was on the hunt to take David's life, yet Jonathan agreed to do whatever David suggested to restore the relationship between David and Saul (20:4) and was faithful to follow through (vv. 12–15). Jonathan had a vision for what David would become. He grieved with David when the relationship with Saul splintered (v. 41) but stayed in touch after David had to flee, helping David find his strength in God (23:16). And David stayed faithful to Jonathan's family long after Jonathan died, keeping his promise to show kindness to the son of his enemy (2 Samuel 9:1).

Isn't Jonathan the kind of friend we all crave? A friend who unequivocally loves us no matter how messy we get or who else comes against us, who makes the commitment to love at all times (Proverbs 17:17)? A friend who sticks by us when life gets hard and keeps checking on us in our most discouraging moments? A friend who stands up for us in front of those who want to demoralize us for the way we're handling life, and who keeps secret the truth of how we're really messing up? Someone who truly fulfills the role of a best man or maid of honor at a wedding by their willingness to step to the side during our shining moment and work out the details to make us shine more brightly?

Though we may not like it at the time, a true friend honestly tells us how we could be better while still loving us as we are. And the best of friends points the way to our one and only best friend—God himself—and challenges us to depend on God, not on other humans.

If you have that kind of friend, you are blessed. If you have a friend with emerging friendship traits, you are still blessed. Hang on to the friendship, for in any relationship, it takes time to cultivate trust. And if you feel, like I often do, that you haven't been the best of friends, start by thanking God for what and who He's given you, lacing the prayer of thanks with a plea that God show you how to be a better bestie.

If the years have stripped away your friends in the flesh, God remains—not merely a bosom buddy with whom you can share secrets and gab over coffee together but the kind of friend who will never leave you in the best or worst of times. He, unlike us humans, will never betray your trust. He is the best of friends.

GRATITUDE PROMPT

List your three closest friends. What do you value about your friendship with each of them? Thank God for placing those people in your life and for how they help you be your best for God.

46

Seasonal Friends

Encourage one another daily, as long as it is called "Today,"
so that none of you may be hardened by sin's deceitfulness.

HEBREWS 3:13

"You're blessed," my aunt told me one day. "Since you don't drive, you have to rely on other people to get you places. That means wherever you go, you share car time with another person, and you always return with such neat people stories. Me? If I want to go anywhere, I pick up my keys and go. Alone."

Well, that's a new perspective. But she is right. Because I must ask for rides, I've met interesting people that have added a rich texture to my life. Some encounters turned into lasting friendships; others have slipped out of my life as easily as they entered.

When I wanted to attend a conference in Kansas City, I asked the registration director if I could carpool with anyone attending from the southern Kansas area. Yes, a woman was coming from Oklahoma City; could I meet her in Wichita? I had never met this woman before, and we lost contact with each other soon after the conference. But for three days, we were inseparable and talked nonstop during the road trip, sharing our life stories, aspirations, and faith in God.

I regretted losing connection with my new friend. I've grieved other lost relationships too. A cross-country move, a misunderstanding, or an overstuffed life caused us to drift apart. Guilt often whispered in my ear: This relationship is worth more than a Christmas card, don't you think?

A speaker at another conference put friendship in perspective. Not every relationship has to last a lifetime. Marriage is the only lifelong relationship the Bible mentions. For one thing, we cannot emotionally sustain deep-level, lasting friendships with everyone. Many times, for whatever reason, we must let a friendship go and move on.

The apostle Paul had many friends—have you noticed? If you read the list of people connections in Romans 16, it sounds like Paul collected names of friends like some children collect rocks. But to Paul, each person was like a precious gemstone, representing a time, place, and memory of someone who had partnered with him in ministry. He described many as "dear friends." Yet since Paul was a man on the move, he couldn't share daily life with all those people. They were face-to-face friends for a season, whose memories Paul cherished the rest of his life.

As we walk through life, God creates intersections between us and other human beings. At each point of contact we have the opportunity to enjoy a particular moment of life with a new human connection. We find reassurance and courage when we walk through a section of life with someone who holds to some of the same values we do. And God uses the diversity of seasonal friends to point us toward a new life direction.

Your friend for an hour might be a fellow tourist at a national park who stands beside you in wonder at God's creation. It might be a weekend night nurse who affirms your belief that God knows and oversees all that is happening. Your new friend could share the floor of a blizzard shelter, and you are grateful God brought someone you could work with to get each other safely home.

Like Paul and Barnabas, you might spend months in good ministry work with a fellow believer, then watch the friendship implode due to a difference of opinion. Despite their eventual disagreement and parting of ways, Paul and Barnabas still had some good ministry years together. Barnabas, whose name means "son of encouragement," was the one responsible for launching Paul into missionary work. His encouragement brought Paul out of hiding and convinced church leadership to accept Paul as a believer and new colaborer.

Ongoing encouragement—that's the purpose behind our short-term friendships. Hebrews 3:13 states that daily encouragement prevents our spirit from being hardened by the deceitfulness of sin. When we engage with people along our life path, we allow God to use them to encourage us, and us to encourage them. Seasonal friends are God's delivery service of His good gifts: they keep our faith strong, inspire us to not give up, and give us examples of how to actively live out our faith. Without any connection with another believer, it would be all too easy to start slipping into habits that don't honor the Lord we love.

Investing in seasonal friendships is worth the effort, even if we recognize the relationship is temporary. If my overarching goal is to distribute God's gifts of hope, joy, peace, and comfort to others, I'll be willing to step out of my routine to initiate connections and seek ways to encourage them as Christ has encouraged me. I'll enjoy the few moments or months we have together, and I'll find ways to appreciate how God has made each of us unique yet so similar.

When you invest yourself in the "Today" of relationships, your life will be richer, fuller, and more directed. And as you revisit life paths that, at the time, seemed strewn with rocks, you'll notice precious gemstones intermingled with the hard moments. The memory of people encounters will bring a smile to your face, and you'll thank God for sending His blessings through someone who came as a stranger but left as a friend.

GRATITUDE PROMPT

Name five people who have blessed your life in some way in the past but with whom you've lost contact. Pause and thank God for the role they have played in your life.

47

Mentors

Join together in following my example, brothers
and sisters, and just as you have us as a model,
keep your eyes on those who live as we do.

PHILIPPIANS 3:17

My fellow students and I called our Christian education
professor "Dr. D." A little in awe of this nationally known
trailblazer in the field of Christian education but being typical
seminary students who needed our moment of levity, we called
her Dr. Deedee behind her back. Once we got to know her as
a friend and colleague, my husband and I finally had the nerve
to reveal her students' nickname for her. She laughed. It was
another sign that Dr. Eleanor Daniel was comfortable in her
own skin.

So comfortable that she introduced a teaching demonstration
one day with these instructions: "Watch what I do and say. Afterward, I want you to tell me what I did right."

How presumptuous, I first thought. But her wisdom became
apparent during the reflection time. After hearing our feedback,
she simply said, "This is what I want you to do when you teach."
She taught us by her example.

Mentoring, also known as disciple making, doesn't have to

be a canned, formal program. While programs give structure for how to entrust our faith to the next generation, we often learn best by watching faith lived out in real time. A Christian mentor is like a life coach that encourages, empowers, and educates you on how to grow in your understanding about God and stay faithful to the end of your life.

That's the kind of relationship Paul had with Timothy, his son in the faith. He invited Timothy to go on his next missionary journey. He put him in leadership over a local group and kept in contact with him through letters. That's why Paul could give the Philippian church the advice to follow his example and others who also modeled his lifestyle (Philippians 3:17). He knew that modeling our faith after good models within our sphere of influence works. Whether a preacher behind a podium or someone in the seat next to us who shares their struggle to reach toward faith, God has surrounded us with people who provide glimpses of what it means to live as a Christ follower.

When I was a teenager, "Grammy Jean" decided to adopt our family. That meant popping over to our house, checking on us each week, and asking questions beyond the expected "How are you?" She freely talked about her devotional life and how she was trusting God for the small things, concepts I'd never heard before from anyone else. She had more health issues than any medical history folder should allow. She dismissed her sleepless, pain-filled nights with a wave of her hand. "If I'm having a bad night, I figure God wants me to spend my time in prayer," she told me, then grinned. "You got prayed for a lot this week."

At the same time, Eugene, a church elder, dubbed himself my official "church dad." He encouraged me, championed me, and gave me jobs to develop my gifts. He also held me accountable. When he discovered that organizers for a charity-sponsored walk-athon had altered my mileage record, and that I was implicit in the deception, he was not happy with me, and he let me know it. But that didn't break our relationship. He kept including me in family gatherings and gave me new challenges.

Mentors step outside the door of the church with us after the weekly worship service and connect with us in off hours so they can guide us in our Christian walk. They permit us to see their personal lives, running the risk that we might uncover the flaws in their faith. Yet during the process, they demonstrate how to live what the Bible teaches and how to do it when the stakes go up. They don't merely tell us. They show us. They tell their stories of struggle and share their aha! moments when they witness God at work.

Jean and Eugene probably never knew the extent to which their words and actions impacted me or the hope they imparted to me as I watched them overcome their own tough moments. They faithfully and consistently guided me through my poor choices when they probably despaired that I could be anything better than I was. But I'll never forget that I learned from Eugene the need for integrity and honesty in my life regardless of the extenuating circumstances. And from watching Jean, I now know how to retain faith despite multiple health issues. In fact, the weaker Jean's body became, the stronger her faith grew. If Jean can do it, so can I.

As you've read about Dr. Deedee, Grammy Jean, and Eugene, what names and faces from your own life come to your mind? What life lessons have they taught you? How did they live the truths of Scripture that caused you to think, Ah, that's how it works! Who taught you to pray, memorize Bible verses, overcome an addiction through God's power, or endure a hard season through dependence on God? Who has modeled forgiveness, grace, honesty, or unconditional love? If you are who you are today because God placed these special people in your life, thank God for them.

Better yet, we can live out the saying, "Imitation is the greatest form of flattery." A godly saint will smile when they see someone for whom they've prayed during many overnight hours now walking with the Lord. As the apostle John wrote, "I have no greater joy than to hear that my children are walking in the truth" (3 John 1:4).

Perhaps the best way to thank your mentors is to live the kind of life in Christ they've modeled for you.

GRATITUDE PROMPT

Thank God for the mentors He has brought into your life who have modeled faith and God's unfailing love to you.

48

The Boss

Whatever you do, whether in word or deed,
do it all in the name of the Lord Jesus, giving
thanks to God the Father through him.

COLOSSIANS 3:17

My boss is mean. She expects my work to be perfect. She loads jobs on me beyond my pay grade. She hounds me if I'm not at my desk by a certain hour. She even makes me take out my own trash.

Wait a minute. I'm a sole proprietor. My boss is me.

In addition to my work-at-home job, I hold the role of manager of my kitchen. I came to a new appreciation for the difference between running my own kitchen and putting myself under the authority of a kitchen manager when I spent two weeks as a short-term worker at a Bible training center in eastern Europe. For once, I didn't have to figure out what to have for supper or care about how much something cost. I didn't have to juggle work schedules or cope with outside interruptions. All I had to do was follow directions. At any given moment, I was only responsible for one little task. It was rather nice. And it gave me a new respect for the loads employers and supervisors often carry.

Gratitude for one's boss comes easy when the boss is reasonable, competent, and gracious. Even then, in other jobs that I've had, I found it easy to complain and blame the boss for frustrations and hitches, especially when coworkers decided to have Roasted Boss for lunch. Emotions and public opinion held reign over rationality, and suddenly I found myself becoming irritable at my supervisor for stuff outside her job description.

I once asked an elder in our church who worked in middle management how a Christian could be a witness for Jesus in the workplace. One item on his short list surprised me: don't join the rumor mill. "Respectfully discuss problems with a supervisor instead of spewing venom to coworkers," he told me.

By now, you've probably guessed how to combat negative reactions to work problems—flip your perspective and list the positive. On your list, include ways your boss or supervisor tries to help ease your workload or make your job a joy. Most folks are doing the best they can. Think about what your supervisor does that you don't have to do. And if certain protocols still bother you, thank God that He has given you ways to pray for your boss. Perhaps God has you in that place to be a respectful witness to the power and love of Jesus.

Of course there are corrupt, incompetent, and abusive bosses. The apostle Peter would agree. In the first century Roman culture, when slaves would be considered several steps below today's minimum wage employees, Peter told his readers in that position to submit to both considerate and harsh masters (1 Peter 2:18). While today's workers have the freedom to move out of abusive employment situations, the apostle Paul's advice shows us how to deal with the average shortcomings of a supervisor: "Whatever you do, work at it with all your heart, as working for the Lord, not for human masters" (Colossians 3:23). A few verses earlier, Paul gives the attitude we all need to have in the work we do: "Whatever you do, whether in word or deed, do it all in the name of the Lord Jesus, giving thanks to God the Father through him" (v. 17).

Working for the Lord isn't a duty-bound drudgery with an undercurrent of resentment. What I do for Jesus comes out of love, devotion, and gratitude for all He has done for me. That's the sincerity of heart the Bible calls us to have toward our employers. We are devoted to the people around us, even unkind bosses. We care about their best interest and are grateful for what they do in their supervisory role.

Like the rest of us, employers are flawed human beings and are likely improving in their leadership skills as much as we are developing our work skills. If we give them the benefit of the doubt, we may realize they may not be the source of the problem but only one more cog in the wheel of a defective system or bureaucracy.

Some jobs and some employers test the best of our resolve to stay positive and grateful. If you have difficulty coming up with gratitude prompts, ask God to prime your thinking with ideas. Here's a starter list for you:

- You have a job.
- You don't have the stress your boss has. That person must assume a myriad of responsibilities you don't have to do.
- God created your supervisor with his or her unique personality, experience, and gifts.
- God brought you to this place, and He can use you to shine as a light for Him and serve the one over you in Jesus's name.

Someone has to be in charge. We may not always agree with our supervisor's policies. We may chafe at someone's telling us what to do. But God is the one who designed the structure of authority and chains of command, and we can thank Hm for the people who willingly step forward to take leadership.

Anyone in leadership will tell you supervisory work is hard and lonely. You can begin to be an advocate for your boss by thanking God for what he or she does.

GRATITUDE PROMPT

Thank God for your current boss, manager, or volunteer coordinator, and thank God for His purposes in bringing that person into his or her current position. Ask God to show you the distinctive strengths that make your boss effective on the job, and thank God for those strengths.

49

Health-Care Providers

I thank my God every time I remember you.

PHILIPPIANS 1:3

My poor emergency department nurse. She never saw it coming.

After the hospital staff put thirteen stitches above my right eyebrow and x-rayed my sprained left foot accrued from a nasty fall in a hotel parking lot, the nurse entered my cubicle to give me final instructions before my dismissal. "You can drive after twenty-four hours," she said.

My face quivered as I rehearsed the joke I've so often pulled on medical staff about my inability to drive. *Be nice*, I told myself.

She caught my smirk. "What's wrong?"

"I don't want to do this to you."

"What?"

I hesitated. "Well, see, I don't drive because I have a severe vision loss."

She gasped. "I'm sorry." She thought she had offended me by mentioning something I couldn't do.

I waved my hand. "No, no. That's not it. I was going to say that I could hardly wait because I've never driven a day in my life."

She responded so appropriately. She laughed hysterically. "Can I take you to meet some of my other patients?"

On the way home, I mulled over that conversation, trying to imagine the vast array of people that sweet nurse encountered day after day. She witnessed people at their worst, both physically and emotionally, yet she was expected to approach each one with competence laced with compassion. Her job required her to be quick thinking and quick witted, efficient yet patient, to do the expected while managing the unexpected.

Her job and the job of every other health-care provider is constantly about other people. They leave their personal stress at home so they can make the stressful moments of their clientele better. They probably hear a lot about what they've done wrong and get little thanks for what they try to do. Our medical personnel are heroes.

Did I say thank you to the nurse who wiped away my blood and changed my bedsheets? Who cared as much for my comfort as for my treatment? I think I did, maybe two little words flung over my shoulder as a tech wheeled me out the door. In retrospect, it seems rather paltry.

Paul's greeting to his friends in the Philippian church is also appropriate for our health-care professionals. He thanked God every time he thought of them. There's an important difference between thanking a person and thanking God for a person. Thanking God directly for someone adds thought and authenticity to what we say. It makes us pause and ask, "Thank God for what?"

As I start my list, 1 Thessalonians 5:18 challenges me to go deeper with my thanks. "Give thanks in all circumstances." God calls us to thank Him for the doctors who have not met our expectations as well as those who have served selflessly. I found it easy to thank God for the EMTs who came within four minutes of my fall in the parking lot, the ER doctor who apologized that she must make me hurt in order to stitch my head back together, and my sweet nurse who laughed at my clumsy attempt to infuse humor into a tough situation. But I also catch myself comparing doctors. "This doctor is great because he listens to me. He's articulate. He explains things well. But this other doctor?"

Regardless of my provider's bedside manner or minor flaws, I can thank God that I have a doctor to visit, a nurse who showed up for work, office staff willing to partner with me to work through the quagmire of insurance claims, and all these people who persevered through rigorous training. I can express gratitude for the gifts God has given each of them: the skill, personality, and experience that uniquely qualify them to do their job.

When we thank God for the people around us, we'll find gratitude changes us. That, in turn, empowers us to bless others. How does that happen with our health-care providers?

Gratitude reduces your anxiety. Philippians 4:6 tells us, "Do not be anxious about anything, but in every situation, by prayer and petition, with thanksgiving, present your requests to God." You'll find yourself thankful that God has provided people to take care of you rather than feeling anxious about what is physically wrong with you.

Gratitude passes forward the peace of God. The next verse assures us that peace is the outcome of our thanksgiving. "And the peace of God, which transcends all understanding, will guard your hearts and your minds in Christ Jesus" (v. 7). Peace is contagious. Others will notice the difference gratitude has brought about in your life because you will be more relaxed and focused on others rather than the problem at hand, and you won't be so inclined to complain to those serving you.

Gratitude equips you to focus on others rather than yourself. Weaving gratitude into every thought about your provider will inadvertently impact how you communicate with that individual. You'll find yourself treating them as partners rather than adversaries. It will restructure what you say about them to fellow patients and family members. A "thank you" at the end of the visit will come out more spontaneously and sincerely.

Saying thank you to health-care providers is always appropriate, but we'll have a greater impact when we allow gratitude to permeate our entire approach to our medical care team. They need it. God may use your smiling face and gentle words to encourage a health-care worker who may have just dealt with a cantankerous patient or heart wrenching diagnosis.

God uses people to accomplish His will. He brings healing to us through the hands of these gifted professionals. In turn, God can bring healing to hurting hearts when we show genuine expressions of thankfulness to those who serve our physical needs.

GRATITUDE PROMPT

Make a written list of the doctors, nurses, technicians, and therapists you most likely will encounter within the next few weeks. Spend time in prayer, thanking God for each one.

50

Enemies

But I tell you, love your enemies and pray
for those who persecute you.

MATTHEW 5:44

My limited vision has made shopping a struggle, and I often depend on my husband or others to help me through the aisles or the checkout. One evening, Jack wasn't feeling well, so he stayed in the car while I stepped into the discount grocery store. Dimly aware that two young women were following me, I left nose prints on product labels and careened around endcap displays.

As I bagged my groceries, I discovered several items I had not put in my cart. Turning around, I saw the two women standing by the cash registers, looking at me and laughing. They had evidently snuck the items into my cart, counting on the fact that I would not see them.

Believe me, at that moment, they would not have made it on an invitation list to my next party. I was humiliated. And angry.

All of us have encountered people who either don't like us or mistreat us. Our personalities clash. We have conflicting viewpoints. We live different lifestyles. Some intentionally or carelessly hurt us. And then there are corrupt institutions whose broad, sweeping decisions negatively impact our lives and champion causes that oppose all that we value and believe.

Enemy is a strong word. But I can imagine that you, like me, would rather not invite those folks to your next party either. Reading these words may unleash a firestorm of unpleasant memories within you. In your mind's eye, you can see the people who have hurt you standing in a line like a firing squad. Others join them: those who've used you, argued against you, put you down for believing what you do, or made decisions with no concern for how those choices affect you.

It hurts. You suppress the anger, but it still hurts. And I'm going to tell you to thank God for these people?

Before you throw me in front of your own firing squad, let's look at what the Bible says.

Saul, the former king of Israel, was not David's only enemy. David faced off with a giant named Goliath. He fought the Philistines. His son Absalom turned against him. At one point David wrote,

> But my enemies are vigorous and strong,
> And those who wrongfully hate me are many.
> And those who repay evil for good,
> They become my enemies, because I follow
>   what is good.
> (Psalm 38:19–20 NASB)

Jesus told us to love our enemies and pray for those who persecute us. Forgiving is one thing, but continuing to love and pray for them? Yes. And not just a grumbling "Please make them not be jerks" either. As we've discovered, thanksgiving is a part of prayer. If we are to combine gratitude with prayer for people in our lives such as family, church friends, and health care providers, should we not do the same for our enemies?

How can we possibly thank God for those who hurt us? Those

who, in the process of hurting us, also hurt the reputation of the Lord we love?

When my family faced our own lineup of opposition, I reminded my daughters of Paul's words, that our struggle was not against other people but "against the powers of this dark world and against the spiritual forces of evil in the heavenly realms" (Ephesians 6:12). Satan and his evil forces, not the people who oppose us, are our enemy. We can still thank God that He created those specific people with their unique gifts and personalities; that Jesus offers them the same grace He has extended to us; and that, if they are believers, they are growing in the grace and knowledge of Jesus (2 Peter 3:18) just as we are.

It is oh-so-hard to be grateful, but we can also thank God for how our enemies make us stronger. "As iron sharpens iron, so one person sharpens another" (Proverbs 27:17). A different opinion, a questioning of how we do things that feels like criticism, or a sharp disagreement has a way of clarifying where we stand on an issue. Another person's contention calls us to make choices: Do I believe what I believe enough to disagree with someone to the point that they won't like me? That they refuse to be my friend or make me suffer for my conviction? Resistance gauges the strength of our spiritual muscles and makes us stronger in the process.

As Jesus said in Matthew 5:11–12, we can rejoice when people falsely accuse us because of our faith in Jesus. We have begun to suffer like Jesus and the great Old Testament prophets suffered. Persecution shows we're living our faith loud enough for others to notice—and that's a good thing.

Finally, we can thank God for His incredible way of using oppression for greater good. When Joseph reconnected with the brothers who sold him into slavery, he could reassure them, "You intended to harm me, but God intended it for good to accomplish what is now being done, the saving of many lives" (Genesis 50:20). By removing Joseph from his family in Canaan,

God repositioned him to be the leader who brought the known world through a seven-year famine.

Opposition gives us firsthand experience of the truth that God is greater than any evil force in our world. Even if we cannot see how God is working our circumstances for His greater good, we can thank Him that He continues His efforts to win over the one who has opposed and hurt us. God alone has the power to transform and renew anyone, even as He has done for us.

GRATITUDE PROMPT

Make a short list of people who have hurt you, opposed you, or disagreed with you. Pray that God will remind you of one or two facts about that person for which you can thank God. Write what you discover beside each name.

PART SIX

Walking in the Dark

I waited patiently for the LORD;
he turned to me and heard my cry.
He lifted me out of the slimy pit,
out of the mud and mire;
he set my feet on a rock
and gave me a firm place to stand.
He put a new song in my mouth,
a hymn of praise to our God.
Many will see and fear the LORD
and put their trust in him.

PSALM 40:1–3

In the worst of times, we can thank God for who He is, what He is doing, and how He walks through our deepest pain with us.

51

Financial Stress

The earth is the LORD's, and everything in it,
the world, and all who live in it.
PSALM 24:1

As you have read along with me so far, you and I have found
gratitude tucked into five areas of our lives. We've enjoyed
seeing what we already have. We've discovered God's hidden
treasures of goodness by looking at the other side of what the
world terms bad or inconvenient. We've shared smiles over the
stories of what God has done in the past, and we've found new
and exciting depths within the spiritual blessings we have through
Jesus that are forever ours to keep. We've appreciated the people
God has arranged to walk life's journey with us.

Let's make this real. In the worst of moments, when crisis
smashes into an ordinary day, is it possible to stay thankful in
those moments of loss?

Life events have a way of sweeping what we have out the door
and taunting us with what we can no longer call our own. The
most cheerful among us struggle to smile during the catastrophic.
Stories of the past make no sense in the reality of the present.
Spiritual blessings? Don't talk to me about peace. Or justice.
Sheer faith helps me cling to the idea that God is still faithful

when everything screams to the contrary. And we feel so alone, like no one understands.

Jesus is still there. Because of Him, we can be thankful in all circumstances.

Some worst moments explode like an unpredicted tornado, turning the kiss of a dewy morning into the tears of an afternoon's destruction. Other struggles wrap fiery tendrils around the mundane moments of family life, putting us on constant red alert for imminent disaster.

The slow drain is the stuff of financial stress.

You feel always on guard, programmed to take precautions, and constantly wondering when the proverbial other shoe will drop. Financial stress doesn't play favorites among the rich or the poor. Whether our money sits in stocks, the bank, or our pocket, all of us face the challenge of managing our wealth wisely enough to have enough.

Anxiety dwells in the fear of future loss rather than the reality of the moment. Grocery store inflation, higher internet bills, and depleted mutual funds lead us to recalculate our monthly budget. We worry over the possibility of medical emergencies, identity theft, or unexpected household repairs and replacements. Even attempts to figure out the convoluted charges on a cable bill leave us muttering, "It would be nice to not have to think about money."

I felt that way one first Monday of April. As our custom, Jack and I reviewed our financial status for the last month. It had been a quiet month, and we had been extra conservative, able to save a bit.

"We're fine unless something big happens," Jack said.

How big? I wondered. A dental bill had erased the gain two months before. Every week, I prayed over our derelict washer and dryer. On this day I was on my way out the door to a specialist's appointment that would be a hefty self-pay.

As I rode to my doctor's visit I prayed over our finances,

wishing we could have a bigger margin to make purchases we kept putting off. "If only I could land that contracted work I applied for," I told God.

Who was I to tell God how to do His job? Wasn't my lavishly creative Lord capable of coming up with His own possible solutions? Why limit Him to my paltry idea of a temporary work assignment? Wasn't He adept at solving the big financial stresses with a bigger story?

When we define how God ought to solve our problems, we set ourselves up for disappointment when He doesn't deliver according to our terms. But when we ask Him to provide in ways only He can and in the way He sees as best, He may surprise us with a solution we never would have thought up on our own. And His bigger and better ideas cause gratitude to burst forth in excited praise.

That's exactly what He did that first Monday of April.

The doctor's receptionist told me I had an account credit, and there was no charge for that day's visit. That afternoon, our tax preparer informed us of a substantial tax return. Neither made sense. But it didn't have to make sense. God showed us He was taking care of our financial needs.

The Lord is the owner of all the earth. He made it; therefore it belongs to Him—all of it, including whatever has come under our care. Anything we have is not really ours. It is His and only ours to manage. We are His beloved children, and He's promised He will provide for us (Philippians 4:19), giving us what we need when we need it. And at the same time, His unlimited wisdom offers us ways to prioritize what is important in life and gain an eternal perspective that allows us to be content with where we are at the moment. His provision for our financial needs become portraits of His faithfulness to His children.

Of course I thanked God for that medical credit and tax return. But I forgot to thank Him with equal enthusiasm *before* I left for my appointment. We can turn worry into worship when we look at our bundle of financial stressors and say, "Lord, I don't know how You are going to do it, but I thank you for providing my family with what we need. I thank you for doing it in such a way that it gives us a story to tell that will honor You."

As we learn to thank Him for how He will take care of us, the stress dissipates. He's in charge, not us. He will ensure that we have all we need.

For that, I'm grateful.

GRATITUDE PROMPT

What financial stresses do you currently face? Thank God that He knows what you need and that He will provide for you.

52

Job Loss

She gave this name to the LORD who spoke to
her: "You are the God who sees me," for she said,
"I have now seen the One who sees me."

GENESIS 16:13

Many families live one step from the edge of financial fallout.
Then the Something Big happens. One wage earner comes
home with a file box and a termination slip.

I've lost a job. But I was happy about it. I had a part-time job
during graduate school as a file clerk. I didn't like the work, I
wasn't good at it, I was bored out of my mind, and I never connected with my office mates. Newly married and in the final year
of graduate degree work, I had my mind on other things. Without
a boring job to drag me down, I could focus on writing my thesis
and pampering my husband who, in the meantime, got a much
better full-time job. See? God must have meant it for good.

But I've had dear friends who loved their job, were good at what
they did, had been at their company for decades, made lifelong
friends at the coffee stand, and then got a dismissal notice. We
shared their grief, confusion, hurt, and fear.

Job loss is a composite crisis, one big loss that encompasses
many fragments of stress. Beyond worry over financial survival

until you can find a new job, other emotions war within your heart. There's a sense of betrayal by a company that should have treated you better. You begin questioning your value and capabilities. A self-abasing litany runs laps in your brain: Wasn't I good enough to keep? Maybe I'm not good enough for the next job. After all, who wants someone who has been fired? I hate the learning curve of something new. Job relocation means change, and I don't like change.

We feel alone, unworthy, and scared. Our heads and other people tell us God might have something better in the future, but that's hard to accept on your first day at home, staring at the LinkedIn screen. Does God really understand?

Two Bible people would—Hagar and Joseph. Hagar, Sarah's Egyptian maid, got the pink slip twice from her mistress. Hagar probably deserved the dismissals, but neither incident was solely her fault. The first time, she copped a superior attitude toward Sarah because Hagar had become pregnant with Abraham's child, not Sarah. The second time, Hagar's son, Ishmael, made fun of Isaac, the son God had promised to Abraham and Sarah for so many long years. Hagar was sent on her way into the wilderness where she sank in despair.

Both times, God met her and made promises to her that her offspring would become a great nation. Hagar's reaction is beautiful. She coined a descriptive name for God: the God Who Sees, for "I have now seen the One who sees me" (Genesis 16:13).

Three generations later, Joseph, already betrayed by his flesh-and-blood brothers, lost his job as house manager for a rich man and was sent to prison under the false charge of raping his employer's wife. He languished in prison for several years before God brought him forth to create a plan for famine relief that would save the Egyptians and the surrounding countries. When his brothers asked for his forgiveness for selling him into slavery in the first place, Joseph told them, "You intended to harm me, but God intended it for good to accomplish what is now being done, the saving of many lives" (50:20).

Looking at the stories of Hagar and Joseph, how can we stay thankful in between jobs? Hagar gives us our first prompt: Like Hagar, realize that God sees us. He sees what has happened to us. He knows the why behind our dismissal far better than we do. He knows us intimately, how He has created us to be, and He sees all that He has prepared for us in the future. We can say with confidence, "Thank you for being the God who sees."

Second, your employer may have been unjust, unfair, or malicious. But as God did with Joseph, He will expertly turn the worst into the best. Losing your job may be God's way of moving you into position so you can take hold of what He has next for you. That might be hard to accept at the time, but faith provides the confidence to thank God for what He will do. We can say, "Thank you, Lord that you have already prepared my future, whatever that might be. Thank you for the opportunity to walk with You in the meantime and witness how You will take care of me until and after You have me where You need me to be."

Telling God thank you puts feet on your trust that He will guide and provide. While you wait for His next direction, you may have to pray the same prayer of thanks every day, sometimes every hour. But those words of thanks will cement in your soul that He is full of goodness, wisdom, and unfailing love for you, and He will keep His promises to bring His best to you.

GRATITUDE PROMPT

Are you in the middle of a season of life change due to a job loss? Start a list of how God has already provided for you, how He is with you in the present, and how He will be true to His character in caring for you in the future.

53

Conflict

Blessed are the peacemakers, for they
will be called children of God.

MATTHEW 5:9

I sat across from a dear friend, too full of pain to express the
hurt I felt from the matter that had come between us. Church
members had made some decisions that directly impacted our
family without consulting us. I finally spoke the words, and she
shook her head. She didn't understand. From her perspective,
the church wasn't doing anything unusual, and they had not
intended to hurt us.

The conflict, we determined, wasn't worth the corrosion of
our strong friendship. We both kept sharing our perspectives,
and finally she nodded. "We didn't know the impact this would
have on you as a family. But now I do. Thank you for telling me."

We all face conflict to various degrees. Tensions arise from
differences in opinion, annoyance over a housemate's quirky
habits, hurt over the consequences from another's poor choices, or
simply a misspoken or misunderstood word in a cranky moment.
Conflict erupts when either party has strong opinions about their
position or feels the passionate need to set things right, or—let's
be honest—when we want our way.

Sometimes we are at direct odds with someone. At other times we walk into the middle of a verbal fistfight, wondering if we should break it up or pass the popcorn and enjoy the show. The issue might run the gambit from silly to serious, where each person has a valid point—just a different perspective.

Hold up, you might be thinking. Isn't conflict wrong? Didn't Jesus pray for unity (John 17:20–23)? Aren't we supposed to "make every effort to keep the unity of the Spirit through the bond of peace" (Ephesians 4:3)?

It would be wonderful if we all agreed or always deferred to what the other wanted. But Jesus and Paul never meant for us to be a homogenous people. That's impossible. All of us have different gifts, skills, experiences, and personalities. Sometimes those differences rub against each other like the quills of porcupines seeking warmth from each other on a cold winter's night.

Differences are not wrong. Conflict exists because we live in a fallen world, whether we started it or walked into the middle of it. Conflict is resolved by how we choose to handle tension when perspectives clash.

Surprisingly, the Bible contains many stories of people who quarreled with each other. The servants of Abram and Lot argued over pastureland. Jacob and Laban were at odds about wages, possessions, and Jacob's desire to go back to Canaan. And the great apostle Paul had a falling out with his missionary partner, Barnabas, over the inclusion of the deserter John Mark.

This is a book about being thankful in the tough times. I imagine you're thinking, Are you seriously going to say I need to be thankful for conflict?

Yes. I am. The Bible shows how God can use conflict to bring about His plans and purposes.

My favorite example of conflict handled right is found in the book of Philemon. Onesimus, a slave, apparently stole from his Christian master, Philemon, and ran away. Somehow Onesimus connected with Paul and became a Christ follower. Paul wrote a gracious letter to Philemon, asking him to take back Onesimus and treat him like a Christian brother. Paul didn't allow the clash between master and slave to trump his relationship with Philemon. In fact, he writes, "I always thank my God as I remember you in my prayers" (Philemon 1:4). Paul was confident that Philemon would do the right thing and it would be a win-win for everyone. How can God use conflict for our greater gain?

Conflict gives us an opportunity to practice forbearance, patience, and unconditional love at a higher level.

Conflict tests the tensile strength of our relationship. Will we allow the conflict, no matter how big or small, to weaken our love and respect for the other person?

Conflict mirrors our weaknesses and shows us where we need to grow (or grow up). It allows us to exercise self-control over our emotions so we don't turn the expression of differences into a dispute that explodes out of control (Proverbs 17:14). And in rationally discussing those differences, we and our opponent sharpen each other and grow stronger in the process (27:17).

Conflict challenges us to articulate and examine our opinions, perspectives, and priorities. It calls us to choose what's worth championing and what we need to let go of for the greater good.

Conflict invites us to participate as a peacemaker. As a Christ follower, we can model forgiveness, wisdom, rational thinking, and kindness for those caught in conflict.

Each of us have different emotional reactions to relational tension or disputes. Like so many other struggles in life, God can take the worst situations and bring beauty from them. Because we know God has the power and willingness to bring good and healing out of woundedness, we can react to impending conflict by thanking God for this opportunity to make peace. We can thank Him for making each of us unique people and for this chance to grow through hardship so we'll come out stronger on the other side. And we can thank Him that He chooses to use us to reflect His patience, forgiveness, peace, and unfailing love.

Thanking God for a conflict happening to you right now might be very difficult. Take the challenge to thank God that He gives you this chance to pursue peace and lead others to do so as well.

GRATITUDE PROMPT

What relationship conflict do you currently face? Write it on a piece of paper, then list how you can be thankful for that conflict.

54

Separation

Surely I am with you always, to the very end of the age.
MATTHEW 28:20

Where did my mother go?
On a warm spring day, my mother came to stay with me while the electricity was shut off at the home where she lived with my sister. Mother's dementia was in full reign that day. She repeated stories and asked the same questions at least five times each. Her barbed, unfiltered comments made me grit my teeth.

Where was the woman I once knew—the strong, independent, opinionated woman who showed her love more by what she did than what she said? She was dematerializing before my eyes, replaced by this bent, frail stranger. We would have precious moments of normalcy and then it would seem like her mind furtively slipped out of the room and a woman I did not know took her place.

Separation comes in as many colors as a skein of variegated yarn. Some happen slowly, like a car pulling out of your drive, the person you love waving a slow goodbye out the side window. Other losses feel like someone has been ripped from your embrace, leaving gaping, bleeding holes in your heart. Yet others, like my mother's battle with dementia, flit from tree to tree in your yard, appearing briefly, talking even less, and disappearing again behind the next tree, soon to be seen no more.

Loss, no matter through death, a move to another state, the scimitar-sharp stab of suicide or divorce, or a stormy end to a friendship, feels like an invisible pair of scissors has severed the bonds between you and what you once held close. We look across the wide gulf that stands between us and that person's retreating back, realizing we can no longer touch, speak, or listen to his or her voice again. What child has wanted to call a parent for advice on a cooking project, car maintenance, or raising a recalcitrant teenager, only to remember, "Oh yeah. They're gone." Then there are those relationships that are dead while both persons yet live. Divorce, a shattered friendship, an emotional drifting while under the same roof . . . the longing to connect is strong; the prohibition, heart-wrenching.

Lest we hold too tightly to those God has placed in our inner circle, it does us well to remember that no relationship on this earth is permanent. Life is fleeting, the Bible tells us, using the imagery of grass withering on a hot summer's day (Isaiah 40:6–8). All too true, but there are days I don't like withered grass. Not one bit. Wilted life reminds me of my own mortality and tempts me to not build strong relationships in the first place because the pain is too great when I look at what once was but is no more.

But it's the finale of that passage in Isaiah that reminds us of what does last and what we can cling to in gratitude: "The word of our God endures forever." The words of the Bible further reassure us of the enduring natures of God's presence and promises. To God, a day is like a thousand years (2 Peter 3:8). In this life, Jesus promised He would be with us always (Matthew 28:20). And the Shepherd's Psalm assures us that we will dwell in the house of the Lord forever (Psalm 23:6).

How does this help us stay thankful when separation removes those we love? If we place our dependence on God, find our identity in Him, and make our connection with Him the key relationship in our life, we won't be as prone to become dependent on the strength of our earthly relationships. When others leave, we remain tethered to God. He is the only lifeline that cannot be severed through death, divorce, conflict, or neglect. He is always with us, always there for us. He will never abandon us, and nothing in this world can separate us from His love for us.

God gives us the people in our lives to encourage us, walk the journey of life with us, and give us joy. But God never intended for people to replace Him. When separation's grief and longing threaten to consume us, we can lift our drooping heads and thank God that He is still there. Knowing we'll always have God reduces the pain of any earthly separation. It doesn't remove the pain, but it does reduce it.

Human relationships are important. For that reason, God gives us memories of past pleasant moments that assuage the loss. The Christ follower finds comfort in the knowledge that separation is short-term, and a goodbye is more of a "see you later." We will dwell in the house of the Lord forever, and those who have loved our Lord will stand beside us once more.

Loss and longing are part of life's ongoing struggles that can catch us off-guard in the most unpredictable moments. We regain our balance by thanking God for the "see you later" promise and for His reassurance that, in the meantime, He is our constant companion, the One who is still here and isn't going anywhere.

GRATITUDE PROMPT

Whom do you miss? Thank God for that person's life and how he or she connected to your life. Thank God that He is with you always, knows about the separations of your life, and has promised the hope of "see you later."

55

Culture Clash

The apostles left the Sanhedrin, rejoicing because they had
been counted worthy of suffering disgrace for the Name.

ACTS 5:41

When we moved to North Carolina, the locals figured out
I wasn't a Southerner before I could open my mouth to
betray my Midwestern accent. The tattletale was the jug of un-
sweet tea I brought to a church potluck.

"How do you stand that stuff?" a teenager asked.

My response? "Very well, thank you."

Christ followers encounter culture clash too. Our choice to
live in obedience to Jesus sets us apart in many revealing ways.
We talk and act different. We advocate different perspectives and
choose alternate entertainment. We have distinctive views about
relationships, politics, wealth, and the treatment of people. It's
enough to make us feel more of a misfit than a Midwesterner in
a Southern culture. By the very nature of the transformed life,
we would make lousy undercover agents.

I felt the clash of my Christian faith the day a stranger dumped
a used recliner out of his truck onto my curb. I ran out of my
house. "What are you doing?"

He shrugged. "Someone bought this at a garage sale down the
street and asked me to deliver it." He had the right address, but

I insisted I had not bought that recliner. Help me stay calm and kind, I implored my heavenly Father. Finally the man loaded the recliner into his truck, using foul language that made my heart blush.

If I were raised differently, I would have dished back a few choice words of my own. For me, the greater temptation was to stick my finger in his face and tell him that, as a God-fearing woman, I was highly offended by his foul words. But my faith in the grace of Jesus calls me to a higher standard. A third option came to mind that better reflected my faith-walk: Love him unconditionally, no matter how he acts. Be firm but kind—the one standing before you is more important than a silly recliner. And (gulp) pray for him.

I walked into my house, brain weary. Life would be easier if I didn't have to waste mental moments processing three ways to interact with any one person. Paying forward the grace of Christ takes extra work, and work takes energy.

In times like these, I appreciate the unlimited strength and wisdom available to me through the indwelling of the Holy Spirit. The tension between my faith and the world's ways may be stressful, but God gives me the resiliency and resources I need to deal with it. And I find it reassuring that my inner mental workout is proof that the Holy Spirit is working within me. There was a day when I would have matched the man's anger or fumed about his rudeness to the next available person, fantasizing of creative ways to inform him where he could go with his foul words and dingy recliner. The fact that I asked God's partnership in portraying grace and kindness gave evidence of my buy-in to love others as Christ has loved me.

It's uncomfortable to be the abnormal one, whether it's in our selection of tea, our refusal to embrace a trending lifestyle choice, or our restraint of zippy but equally nasty retorts. The world will not react favorably when we model righteousness and confidence in God's truth. In fact, Jesus warned that the world will hate us for whom we've become (John 15:19). We represent what they know they should be, so they may lash out in anger and argument. It won't always be about the main thing—the reality of Jesus. Instead, the clashes will pop up like rain squalls and funnel clouds over the little stuff: words, habits, choices, and views about current events expressed at social gatherings.

God calls us to represent His kingdom as if we were ambassadors in residence on behalf of the leader of a foreign country (2 Corinthians 5:20). As an ambassador, we enter a culture quite different from our own with the mandate to stay true to the One we serve. The differences are as stark as night and day, for Paul reminded his readers that we "shine among them like stars in the sky as you hold firmly to the word of life" (Philippians 2:15–16). And when others sneer at us for not acclimating to current culture, we can cling to the inner contentment of a student who quietly earns a high grade on a class project. Their mistreatment shows us that someone noticed our different lifestyle and that God has counted us worthy to suffer disgrace for His name.

As a Christ follower, you will clash with your culture. You will need to make the hard choice to resist the urge to be like everyone else. When you feel the tension, thank God that He is there to help you overcome and, in the process, influence others with the gospel and love of Jesus. Light works best when it shines in dark places. Cool water serves best those who thirst the most. Stand firm and praise God that He chose you to be a distributor of His light and living water. You are refusing what the world has because you have something far better waiting for you in God's eternity, something of greater value to share with them.

GRATITUDE PROMPT

When did you last feel the tension of following Jesus among those who do not follow Him? Thank God that the tension marks you as one who belongs to Jesus.

56

Weather Woes

By this everyone will know that you are my
disciples, if you love one another.

JOHN 13:35

Weather disasters have a way of bringing out both the best
and the worst of people. It's the best that salvages the
destruction and salves the damaged memories of horror and loss.
It seems bizarre. How can good be birthed from the worst?
Yet God is expert at accomplishing just that. That's what Jesus's
resurrection is about—bringing life out of death. His transformation of sin-spotted lives proves He can morph condemnation
into grace. And devastation caused by hurricanes, tornadoes, and
blizzards? A perfect opportunity for God to work through His
people to bring restoration and healing; to whisper, "Peace! Be
still" into the fears and griefs of those who have suffered.

I've hidden behind walls in three weather events and emerged
to see an altered landscape. Other times, I've stood at the sidelines
and heard reports from close friends of destruction from the
2007 Greensburg, Kansas, tornado; the 2011 Joplin, Missouri,
tornado; and Hurricane Harvey in 2017. In each event, I heard
stories of individuals and churches speaking the love of Christ
through acts of compassion.

Clovis, a man in our North Carolina church, realized he would lose his freezer food when a straight-line wind downed trees and cut power for a week in 2001. We were to move into our first mortgaged home the day after the storm, so Clovis offered to grill meat from his freezer for our work crew. Our new property had heavy tree damage. A church group worked down our street, cutting up and removing tree limbs and trunks from properties.

A blizzard swirled through Western Illinois the Sunday after Thanksgiving, 2018, stranding dozens of motorists. The local fire chief contacted my preacher-husband: Could they use our church gym as a shelter? The community worked together to ferry people to the church, donate and cook food, and provide blankets for the sixty-seven visitors. One woman walked through the storm to donate dog food for the three dogs in the crowd.

Eight months after an EF5 tornado ripped a mile-wide swath through the center of Joplin in 2011, I visited the town to interview a team from Western Illinois churches who had banded together to raise money and build a home for a widow and her three children after the tornado took everything but the cement garage steps of her home. While there, I heard story after story of people of faith spending unlimited hours and resources helping their neighbors restore and rebuild Joplin. Social and economic status and church affiliation were flung to the side as everyone shared what they had with those who had suffered such tremendous loss.

As Christians, we get to reflect the nature of Jesus to those in need. He calls upon us to bring life from death and offer grace and mercy as He would do. He instructed His disciples, "As I have loved you, so you must love one another" (John 13:34). His word for love is *agape*, that unconditional commitment to love because someone needs it, not because they deserve it. And when we show that depth of love, those watching with upturned longing faces will know with certainty that our faith is real and there is a God who cares.

God's mercy rides the winds of the storm, setting an example for us to follow. My husband entered our new house in North Carolina with an armload of stuff seconds before the straight-line wind hit. As he turned to close the door, a tree trunk sailed past where he had stood, taking out our car's side view mirror. It was God's message to us: As I have loved you, so you must love one another. God had shown his power to rescue, protect, and take care of us. Would we do the same for others?

God has called me to deliver His mercy on the tailwind of storms by offering my basement during a tornado warning to those who didn't have a storm shelter. We've joined cleanup crews that have removed yard waste after a damaging microburst. And like Clovis who shared the contents of his freezer, we've learned to share what we have when the power is off for several days so that everyone in our immediate circle, whether neighbors, family, or church small group, has what they need. Learning to love like Jesus loves has taught me to look at impending storms with a different prayer approach. "Lord, thank you for the opportunities this weather event will give us to reach out to those who need to see how You can provide for them in the midst of this tragedy."

What can we possibly thank God for during a life-threatening storm? We can praise Him that nature's worst allows God to extend His powerful hand of mercy through us. It calls Christians to love as Christ would love and extend grace and mercy to those more ready to listen because of their need. A weather disaster ushers us into the rubble of their homes and the ruins of their hearts. As we stand side by side, facing the aftermath, they get a front row view of the hope we have—that through Christ, we can make it through stronger than ever and that, while the worst may linger, better than ever is yet to come.

GRATITUDE PROMPT

The next time you hear of impending severe weather, thank God for giving Christians the chance to model the mercy of God and proclaim the hope they have in Christ.

57

Chronic Pain

He said to me, "My grace is sufficient for you,
for my power is made perfect in weakness."
2 CORINTHIANS 12:9

Pain is a tyrant.

Chronic pain demands all your attention. It siphons your physical and emotional strength and steals your resources. It takes ownership of your schedule, barging in when you would rather focus on other parts of life. It laughs at your weakness and dangles your freedom before you like a prize of war. It heckles your faith, saying you'll give up on God if the pain increases. It leers that it will win and you will give up on God.

The resulting despair is exactly what Satan wants. He desires to use pain to show God that you can't do this faith thing. "See," he taunts, "I told you that one couldn't stay faithful to you."

That's what happened to Job.

Satan had already asked to test the tenacity of Job's faith by stripping him of all he owned and held dear, including his children. But Job praised God and stayed faithful (Job 1:20–22).

On Satan's next pass through heaven, God asked if Satan had noticed Job. "He still maintains his integrity, though you incited me against him to ruin him without any reason" (2:3).

Satan scoffed. "Strike his flesh and bones, and he will surely curse you to your face" (v. 5). God was so confident about his man that He allowed Satan to go through with the test. And while Job wrestled with not knowing the reason for his pain, and his friends debated the motivation for such a punishment, Job did not capitulate in his belief in a sovereign, good, and enduring God. "I know that my redeemer lives, and that in the end he will stand on the earth" (19:25).

God was right about Job. And He is right about you too. Pain does not have to veto your faith. You can praise God through the pain.

Paul described his source of pain as a thorn in the flesh. Theologians have debated for centuries what the malady was that tormented Paul, but if it's anything like having a splinter protruding through your fingernail or a cactus spine caught on the inside of your knee, I can't imagine how Paul possibly did all that he did through that veil of pain. The apostle's litany of beatings, shipwrecks, and stonings would be enough to land the man in bed with chronic osteoarthritis from head to foot (2 Corinthians 11:23–25). Paul wrestled with his pain issue enough that he begged God to remove it.

Instead, God used that moment to teach Paul—and us—that He is powerful enough to work through our deepest pain. His grace is sufficient. We can make it through, faith intact—through Him.

The world sees those in chronic pain as weak and unproductive. That's not how God views us. He didn't cause the pain; pain is part of the plight of our sin-ravaged earth. But God can use our pain to show how He can bring about strength in character through weakened bodies.

We are not relegated to merely making it through. We not only survive; we thrive! We flourish. God uses us to do His greater work, showing the world that when His work is done by the weak among us, it proves that it came from Him. Through the weakening of our bodies, our spirits gain strength.

The problem of pain becomes a solution in God's kingdom. We show an attentive world, awakened by the clarion call of our pain, that God can reign supreme. We don't have to give in because we know that one day God will remove the pain and invite us to His pain-free world in eternity. Like Jesus, we can fix our eyes on that joy, despising the here and now of the shame and pain we face, and look forward to the time we gather around the throne of God (Hebrews 12:2).

God looks at our pain, illness, suffering, or disability, and says, "Watch what I can do with this for the good of my kingdom." And He invites us to do the same: to use our suffering as a means to proclaim His goodness to those watching us.

Many people in my life have shown me how faith can win over pain. Remember Grammy Jean, who used sleepless nights to pray for other people? Then there's my own husband, who has suffered forty years with increasing back issues. When I asked him what he was thankful for regarding his health conditions, he said, "I'm thankful for my excellent medical staff." He looked at me. "I'm also thankful for someone who keeps me accountable and gives me backrubs."

I promise I didn't pay him to say that.

If you live with chronic pain or with someone in constant pain, you have my compassion. It is tough. I know. You have good days and not-so-good days, and you just wish the pain would go away. Your pain is a big deal. But God is bigger. He does have plans and a purpose for you. You may never fully understand what those might be or how He could possibly use you as you are. But He can. Because He is God and He's good at that sort of thing.

Like Job, you may not understand the reasons behind your pain or God's agenda for you. But you can thank God that He knows, He's walking with you through every moment, and one day, He'll take you to that land that is forever pain free. Until then, He is confident that you won't cave and that your faith, through Him, will stay strong to the end.

GRATITUDE PROMPT

If you have trouble focusing because of pain, use praise music to turn your attention to praising God. Thank the Lord that He is willing and able to keep you strong to the end of your life and that your physical ailments don't have to steal your faith.

58

Loss of Eyesight

I will lead the blind by ways they have not known,
along unfamiliar paths I will guide them;
I will turn the darkness into light before them
and make the rough places smooth.
These are the things I will do;
I will not forsake them.

Isaiah 42:16

I've shared the story of how, after decades of legal blindness, I underwent a surgery that gave me better-than-ever vision in one eye. For the first time, I could see my husband's smile, more than a handful of stars in the night sky, wall art from more than three feet away, and the detailed colors of sunset-gilded clouds.

The day may come when I lose what I've gained. I'm not being melodramatic or panic driven. My original genetic disorder and multiple eye surgeries have left my eyes underdeveloped and fragile. A photo of my left eye could make you wonder if it's an eyeball or a shuddering, disintegrating planet as depicted in sci-fi movies. At this point, my specialist has told me that any more eye surgeries would not be wise because the trauma of surgery, or even a blow to the head, could take away the rest of my vision.

223

There are also the normal risks of aging that could diminish my already marginal vision.

I am overjoyed at the unexpected gift of better vision I received in midlife. To say I'm grateful doesn't begin to express my ongoing delight. But as I catch the wistful looks of friends who are losing their vision, and I remember that my better eyesight is a fragile gift, I have to ask myself, Would I remain as grateful if I lost the rest of my eyesight?

Is it possible to retain a grateful attitude if you lose your eyesight? Your hearing? Your mobility? Your strength and independence? When Paul instructs his readers to thank God in all circumstances (1 Thessalonians 5:18), is he expecting too much?

Here's what I've learned.

My unstable vision has taught me the value of the gift. We can't take eyesight or any of our health for granted. None of it will last forever. Our bodies are headed in a downward spiral toward decay. So as we would find new appreciation for a tattered photo album pulled from the rubble of a tornado, we treasure what we hold in our hands this day. Every day, even eight years after my better-than-ever surgery, I thank God for my eyesight. Today, this day, I can see what I can see. Not like others can. Perhaps not as well as yesterday. But I can see enough. And God has put much in my path to be seen. Today I will delight in all I can see and share that delight with my heavenly Father.

If I lost the rest of my vision, I still have so much else. My eyesight is not the focus of my life—God is. His kingdom work comes first. He has promised that if we seek His kingdom, He'll provide everything else. I—and you, if you face physical loss—still have all the everyday and spiritual blessings He's given that won't fade with time. God invites us to fix our thoughts on what we've gained through Christ, not on what we will lose in this world.

I'm grateful for all that God has given me in my life. Despite

224

my lifelong limited vision, I've lived an incredible life. God has given me far more than I deserve. I could have lost what vision I have long ago. The better-than-ever surgery could have brought a worse-than-before result. I have already experienced more years of usable eyesight than doctors or social workers thought possible.

If I lost vision now, how ungrateful it would sound for me to whine about the loss. I would be like the Israelites who, three days after witnessing God's mighty power to deliver them from the tyranny of Egypt, complained about the quality of the water at Marah (Exodus 15:22–25).

Through my limited eyesight God has shown me His infinite power to do the impossible. My lack has been His opportunity to showcase His glory. It has led to me to do what all of us should do anyway—utterly depend on God instead of ourselves. If God has lavishly provided for me in the past, will He not do it again in the future—no matter how severe the loss? God has proven himself wise enough to guide us through the perils of any change, powerful enough to protect us from our new vulnerability, and loving enough to keep filling our lives with productive activity and using us to be influencers.

My unstable vision makes me long for heaven. My current gift of improved eyesight has given me a glimpse that better-than-ever is possible. If I have seen so much more from one small surgery, what will I see in heaven, where normal earthly vision would be considered a disability? We will all see Jesus as He sees us, and we'll see beyond the seen to the unseen. The light will be incredibly bright, seemingly unapproachable. But God will invite us to approach as He welcomes us to our eternal home.

If you face the potential loss of physical strength, eyesight, or other declining health, please don't think I am uncompassionate. I know it's scary and stressful. None of us like to feel helpless, restricted, dependent, or vulnerable. Change is threatening, and some days I feel like I'm getting too old to try to adapt any more.

But concern over our future does not have to lessen our love for God or change our appreciation for all He has done.

We can stay faithful till the end because we know He will stay faithful to us. He will guide us along paths we cannot see, and He will never abandon us.

GRATITUDE PROMPT

Thank God for the eyesight you have today. Look around you. Take note of and thank God for what you can see.

59

Terminal Illness

For to me, to live is Christ and to die is gain.
PHILIPPIANS 1:21

Georgia was the life of any party. Vivacious, positive, and adventurous, Georgia always had a smile on her face and a story to tell. She could turn the worst of life's tragedies into a story that left us smiling. When she broke her foot a year before her death, she loved to laugh over how the silly accident happened.

Life had not been easy. Multiple marriages that ended through either death or divorce. Estranged children. Yet Georgia kept going, always welcoming, interested in others, and never running out of stories.

Then Georgia received the diagnosis of terminal cancer.

Pastor Jesse went to visit and expressed his sorrow and dismay.

"Stop it," Georgia said. "God has given me a good life, and I have heaven waiting. No sorrow!" She was determined that the label of terminal illness would not steal her joy. In fact, Georgia seemed more renewed by her joy and anticipation of heaven.

With the backdrop of my faith in God, the phrase *terminal illness* sounds odd to my ear. I know what it means—an illness for which there is no cure. This is it. This is the illness that will end your life. Yet for Georgia and other Christians, death is not terminal. Death is not the end. It's the beginning of forever. The end of death is life. After this illness, there will be no more sickness, pain, tears, or heartache.

Why wouldn't Georgia be joyful?

This upside-down joy can be true for anyone who puts their trust in Jesus. For the Christ follower, even impending death doesn't have to diminish our thanks. God has walked with us throughout our lives, and He will continue to walk with us to the finish line and then usher us into His everlasting presence.

Still don't feel too excited about heaven? Let's discover what we can be excited about.

In Hebrews 4, the author compares the idea of heaven to a rest period. He reminds us that God created the world in six days and then on the seventh day rested from all He did. Yet verse 3 says this: "And yet his works have been finished since the creation of the world." The seventh day was the beginning of a new era, one of completion. The writer then talks about a Sabbath-rest that is yet to come, a time when we will enter this new phase of rest.

God structured the work week to remind us of what's coming. We work six days and then we rest. The day of rest is a time for worship, but it's more. It's a constant reminder that someday we will enter an eternity of weekends. Friday is over. Sunday's coming. No more Mondays!

Eternal rest ushers in the time when we will always be with the Lord to enjoy the splendors of heaven. We will gain what we've longed to have throughout our earthly life. Rest. Freedom. Deliverance from physical pain and emotional baggage. Everything set right. All things restored to God's original intention.

No wonder Georgia was excited to go.

Yet something within us clings to this earthly life. The pronouncement "There's nothing more we can do" sucks the air out of the room and makes us gasp, "Wait."

Paul would understand. "What shall I choose? I do not know," he said in his letter to the Philippians. "I desire to depart and be with Christ, which is better by far; but it is more necessary for you that I remain in the body" (Philippians 1:22–24). Paul had unfinished business. His death would impact those left behind and leave a space not easily filled. Paul wasn't being proud. His necessity was a fact. And that's true when anyone leaves this earth. Our leaving does affect those who remain.

But if God has directed all the other details of our lives—our time, resources, and work—then He also asks us to allow Him to be in charge of our transition from earth to eternity. We can find contentment that whatever He decides is fine with us. More time on this earth to represent Jesus to those who don't know Him and encourage those who do? Sure. But time to go to our heavenly home? Whenever you say, Lord. That's better by far.

I'm thankful we do have something better waiting for us. As hard as life might get, we know that a splendid valley lies beyond the most treacherous of mountains. We sometimes grieve because life is tough and frustrating, and we weary of the feelings of brokenness and heartache. Yet we don't grieve like those who have no hope. We know there's something better coming. Something better than we've ever had before. Ever.

You may not be to the point where Georgia stood, ready and eager to be with her Lord. You may struggle to have Paul's outlook of "Whatever God decides is fine with me." But you can start your journey toward eager excitement about heaven by simply saying, "Thank you." Thank God that His blueprint includes an eternity of weekends where the labors and struggles of this world will be no more and you'll be forever set free from the clutches of this sin-soaked world.

Heaven awaits, and it will be fantastic.

GRATITUDE PROMPT

What do you look forward most about heaven? Make a list and thank God for the heavenly home He has waiting for you.

60

Only Jesus

In this world you will have trouble. But take
heart! I have overcome the world.

JOHN 16:33

I don't like graphic movies. I go to great lengths to avoid them.
Grisly scenes feel like shattered glass on delicate skin. Clos-
ing my eyes to shut out the blood and gore isn't enough because
I can still hear the soundtrack, and I can't close my ears like I
can my eyes. Knowing my sensitivities, Jack grabs my hand and
allows me to nestle close and then says nothing as I walk out of
the theater. He's gracious enough to say afterward, with a hug,
"It was a good thing you left."

Unfortunately I can't walk out on real life.

I'm deeply grateful I have Jesus. He walks beside me through
the muck. He shelters me from the worst of the worst. He's given
me the protective gear of His truth, wisdom, salvation, faith,
and peace that deflect the Evil One's flaming arrows intended to
destroy my eternal soul.

But how do I know Jesus will keep doing that if my life reel
takes a sharp camera angle to the left and into the ugly? I watch
the feedback loop of those who have gone before me, who have
faced the worst of the worst. They emerge, bearing the scars of

a shattered life and the smell of decay. But they walk upright, praising God, not cursing Him. They still believe He is good, and they are eager to share stories of His watch-care during their darkest moments.

Let me tell you about Julie and Debbie.

These two beautiful ladies stood hand in hand on stage before a large gathering of women. Each had shared incredible stories of heartache, tragedy, and confrontation with evil. The audience wept as we heard nearly unbearable tales of what they had endured. Julie had undergone surgery for a brain tumor, a surgery that forever compromised her immune system. And Debbie had suffered gut wrenching heartache over the murder of her eight-year-old daughter and a thirty-eight-year span of time before justice prevailed.

Yet both women stood tall, strong, and smiling, their faith in Jesus intact and stronger than ever before.

If life strips everything from you, you still have Jesus. If the finger of death flits like an ever-present filament around you, you still have Jesus. And if evil sticks its face in yours to laugh at your repulsion, then steals your dreams of what life on this earth should have been, you still have Jesus. You have the hope He gave you. You can make it through the worst of afflictions and troubles because He will never let you go through it alone.

Your faith will get you through. Yes, you will have to walk through it. None of us is exempt from the hard moments. But we have His promise that if we stall out, He will carry us. He will keep moving us forward till we reach the end of the story and the new beginning of eternity.

"We are hard pressed on every side, but not crushed," Paul wrote in 2 Corinthians 4:8–9, "perplexed, but not in despair; persecuted, but not abandoned; struck down, but not destroyed." You may feel like you're not going to make it. And you can't. Not on your own. But with Jesus, you will make it through.

When the obstacles look like impenetrable boulders and we

can't see heaven's glories, it's hard to fathom how to get through. But Paul promises that the surpassing glories waiting for us in heaven will outweigh any temporary trouble we face here on earth (2 Corinthians 4:17). When we get to heaven, the exhilarating awesomeness of eternity with Jesus will make those boulders look like pebbles.

Maybe you've experienced one of these worst moments:

The untimely, violent death of a loved one.

An encounter with evil: rape, abuse, kidnapping, mistreatment, or physical harm.

A prodigal child or other estranged relationship.

A broken trust: a jagged divorce, or a family member who has stolen from you, lied to you, or pulverized your dreams for the future.

Coexisting beside someone with an addiction.

Caregiving for an elderly parent or child with multiple disabilities that has shoved your life plans into obscurity.

An indictment for something you didn't do, and you've discovered earthly systems of justice are a joke.

All that you've known and loved, for whatever reason, has been wiped from your present moment and disposed of like a piece of unwanted trash.

Debbie and Julie understand. They've walked that path. They found Jesus faithful. While the rest of the world seems unfair and uncaring, Jesus is still there. And when faith and confidence in His trustworthiness becomes the most important thing, all those troubles lose their intimidating edge.

If you have nothing else, you still have Jesus. If you lose everything else, you still have His presence on this earth and His promise of eternal life. You will face trouble, lots of trouble, sometimes what feels like more than your fair share of trouble, but you can face it because you know God's got this. He's in charge. And in the end, He'll win with us at His side, shouting in victorious gratitude.

No matter how much you lose, you will always have Jesus. And Jesus wins. Every time.

In your darkest hour, you can whisper, "Thank you, Jesus, for you."

GRATITUDE PROMPT

Thank the Lord that He has already overcome the world and that He will get you through whatever difficulty you might face in this world.

A Prayer for You

When the worst of moments overtake you, use this prayer to keep your focus on the Lord.

Thank you, God, that . . .

You are always with me.

You will be faithful in the future, even as you have proven yourself trustworthy in my past.

You've given me a stage to showcase my faith in front of a watching audience.

You are trustworthy to provide all I need. Even if this crisis strips away my earthly resources, I can depend on you for everything.

Trials provide a chance to find greater value in what I already have.

Difficulties give me the chance to see your priorities from your perspective.

I have this chance to grow and grow strong.

Your plans for me are still unfolding, and the best is yet to come.

You are still in charge.

Thank you, thank you, Jesus. Amen!

renew,
refresh,
reclaim

In a world that disappoints again and again, your
heavenly Father does not. Wherever you are
today and whatever your situation tomorrow,
know on a whole new level that God is with you,
He is for you, and He will never fail you.

Well-loved author, blogger, and women's
ministry speaker, Lori Hatcher is here to help
renew, refresh, and reclaim your confidence
in the rock-solid truths about God.

Our Daily Bread
Publishing.

Get yours today!

GOD HEARS HER.

Seek and she will find

Spread the Word
by Doing One Thing.

- Give a copy of this book as a gift.
- Share the QR code link via your social media.
- Write a review of this book on your blog, favorite bookseller's website, or at ODB.org/store.
- Recommend this book to your church, small group, or book club.

Connect with us. [f] [○]

Our Daily Bread Publishing
PO Box 3566, Grand Rapids, MI 49501, USA
Email: books@odb.org

Love God. Love Others.
with  Our Daily Bread.

Your gift changes lives.

Connect with us. 🅕 🅞

Our Daily Bread Publishing
PO Box 3566, Grand Rapids, MI 49501, USA
Email: books@odb.org